An Encounter with
Pakistan's Reality

I0110754

Satish Verma
Senior Journalist

DIAMOND BOOKS

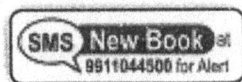

SMS New Book at
9911044500 for Alert

ISBN : 978-81-288-3852-1

© Author

Translated from Hindi by: Anoop Kumar

Publisher	:	**Diamond Pocket Books (P) Ltd.**
		X-30, Okhla Industrial Area, Phase-II
		New Delhi-110020
Phone	:	011-40712100, 41611861
Fax	:	011-41611866
E-mail	:	wecare@diamondbooks.in
Website	:	www.diamondbooks.in
Edition	:	2025

An Encounter with Pakistan's Reality
By - *Satish Verma*

Dedicated to the most respected Eminent
social worker, freedom fighter and father
Babuji Late Shree H.P Verma.

A Word from a Well-wisher

Author Satish Verma has successfully sketched the painful mirror image of Azad Kashmir and Gilgit Baltistan through this book An Encounter With Pakistan's Reality.

Since 64 years, Pakistan have been ruling Pakistan Occupied Kashmir and specially Gilgit Baltistan as its colony. Gilgit Baltistan region have not been given political status as have been given to so called Pakistan Occupied Kashmir.

Satish Verma is credited to be the first journalist, who have penned down the facts, he came across during visit of Pakistan and Pakistan Occupied Kashmir. He got an opportunity to visit even Gilgit Baltistan, where no Indian ,specially Indian journalist visited earlier.

This book is an authentic document of extreme of exploitation faced by migrated Indians tumbling in Pakistan and Pakistan Occupied Kashmir. Satish Verma has remained a journalist with revolutionary mind since beginning of his career. I am happy to see him writing fearlessly.

Professor Bhim Singh
Chairman
Panther's Party (India)
and
Analyst on Jammu and Kashmir Affairs

Foreword

It gives me immense pleasure to congratulate Mr. Satish Verma, senior journalist, for writing the book *An Encounter with Pakistan's Reality*. This is the English version of a book in Hindi (on the same topic) written by Satish Verma.

Satish Verma has created space for himself in the journalist circles with his writings throughout the globe. He has worked hard in the militancy- prone state of Jammu & Kashmir for over two decades. He has a lot of experience in this field. This book assumes importance in view of the strained Indo-Pakistani relationships. I hope that this book will help in normalization of relationships between India and Pakistan, especially between the civil societies of both these countries. These two societies have been the worst suffers due to many reasons. I hope that *An Encounter with Pakistan's Reality* will surely add another feather to the writer's cap. It would also normalise the relationships between the two nations, who belong to the same society.

I extend my compliments and good wishes to Satish Verma. May he continue to be as prolific in his writing as he in his professional journalistic duties! Amen!

Sohail Kazmi
Editor Daily Taskeen
Secretary General
Press Club of Jammu

An Encounter With Pakistan's Reality

A Narration of Cold Reality of Untouched Aspects of
the Most Blasting Indo-Pakistani Issue "Kashmir"

Satish Verma
Senior Journalist
Sahara Samay, Hindi News Channel, Delhi
Former Chief Bureau
Rastriya Sahara, J&K (India)

The Truth

Being Journalist I got an opportunity to visit Pakistan and Pakistan occupied Azad Jammu and Kashmir not only once but twice. Those were not a simple journey but an encounter with the reality of Pakistan. There I clearly understood the false propaganda of Pakistan that Azad Jammu and Kashmir ever wanted to be a part of Pakistan. What a farce and fabricated propaganda! If we talk about the wish and will of common citizen of Pakistan and PAKISTAN OCCUPIED KASHMIR, it is clearly visible that they dream about restructuring of Jammu and Kashmir and a better relationship with India. But there I also found well targeted and fully equipped training centers engaged in the production of hard core fundamentalists. Those training centers were located in the nearby hills and forests surrounding line of control. Probably due to this reason the ISI and Army of Pakistan were trying hard to keep us away from those training centers. Though few people in very disguise manner opened their hurts and accepted that training centers of hardcore terrorists organizations like Lashkare-Toiba, Hisbul Muzahiddin, Pir Panjal and many other exist there and have been operating their centers for years. I understood why entire area was so sensitive.

— Satish Verma

Introduction

At present Pakistan is encircled with such a hurricane that not only disturbs India but also hammers its own people. Terrorism has created an immense fear into the minds and hearts of common people of Pakistan. They hardly believe that they will come back their homes after day's work. Farukh Ahmed is also facing this deadly situation. He is a resident of Lahore and had visited Delhi with his one and half year son for treatment. There was a hole in the heart of his little child. As we all know that medical treatment is very costly in the countries like America and Britain, so Farukh Ahmed found India within his reach as India provides best possible treatment in very reasonable cost. With the grace of Allah (God) son of Farukh got best treatment and became fully cured. But today Farukh is more sad, he finds terrorism making deep holes in the hurt of their nation and this has become a continuous process. Who will fill these holes? Every Pakistani is suffering from these holes. Farukh Ahmed wants to see India and Pakistan in a better relationship. He thanks Allah and expresses his view that lakhs of Pakistani can be treated in India as his son was treated, but it can not be possible without better relationship. Still Farukh Ahmed carries a hope that blessings of millions of Pakistani will make India and Pakistan a true friend. Actually at present Pakistan is facing danger of such volcano that can erupt any moment. I realized this fact during my visit to Pakistan, Northern Pakistan and Azad Jammu and Kashmir. After discussing with various thoughtful personalities on Ground zero, I came on conclusion that coming years would be very difficult for Pakistanis. An era of downfall has already started. Pakistan has become the homes of hardcore fundamentalists and various terrorist groups. This is the most dangerous situation for Pakistan. I have seen one more picture of Pakistan when Miyan Nawaz Sharif were the Prime-Minister of a democratic Government and Delhi-Lahore Bus service were started. The then Prime-Minister of India Atal Behari Bajpai had showed the gesture of true friendship and had visited Lahore. There hardcore fundamentalists and terrorist groups had demonstrated violently against Bajpai's visit in Pakistan. Then we saw Kargil war. Here I must mention the incidence that happened with me at Lahore during this visit. I had taken a three wheeler from hotel to go GPO and in between the way, on the Mal Road, people of intelligence department tried to abduct me.

After the gap of five years, again I got an opportunity to visit not only Lahore but also Islamabad, Rawalpindi, Muzaffarbad, Gilgit and other places through SAFMA. It was hard to get Visa even for PAKISTAN OCCUPIED KASHMIR and we were getting Visa to visit Gilgit, that was almost impossible in previous years. It was SAFMA Sammelan. Prime-Minister Manmohan Singh just had come in power in India. Pakistan had Army Rule headed by General Parwej Musharraf. Both were trying hard to make better relationship. Here I must appreciate General Parwez Musharraf who made possible to travel the most difficult places and given us opportunity to meet with the various people. We could able to see the reality of Ground Zero and the hardship of those people who crossed the line of control from Jammu and Kashmir (India) with the hope of getting complete freedom but were totally ruined. Their children were begging just to fill their stomach. Not only that people of PAKISTAN OCCUPIED KASHMIR were raising strong voice against Pakistan and were demanding freedom. People had enough anger for those undivided land of Azad Jammu and Kashmir and Northern region that was captured by China. Many other sensational facts were also revealed. I revealed some of the facts through our Rastriya Sahara Hindi News Paper. Pakistan was trapped in its own weaved net of terrorism. We had seen its reflection there. We also had seen the magical beauty of nature and felt the immense love of the local people for us and India at large. But the colour of religious war and mysterious silence of people had raised many questions. Probably I was getting answer from the assassination of Salman Tasir, the then Governor of Punjab (Pakistan).

I collected all these facts, took blessings of my mother Taravati Sharma, a great social worker and freedom fighter, and with the help of very close friends Vinod Kumar Sharma, Rajesh Kaushik, Rajesh Sharma, Jatinder Stephen, and Narendra Bhandari I recollected memories of both the visits of Pakistan, and with great efforts of my brothers Sunil Verma and Om Prakash Verma written this book **"An Encounter With Pakistan`s Reality"**. I have all the admiration for the Chairman of Diamond Books Shree Narendra Kumar verma who took great interest for the publication of this book. It was really challenging to edit a book that was based on blasting issues of Indo-Pakistani and also had sensational facts of LOC and PAKISTAN OCCUPIED KASHMIR. Mr. I.M Rajswi, editor of Diamond Books did this excellent job and I have all the praise for him. At last but not least I am here to say that a lot of untouched and sensational facts have been compiled into this book and very first time reaching to its noble readers. Though most of the contents of this book are hard realities, but our motto is to develop better relationship between India and Pakistan despite the facts of Ground Zero. Believing in God that things will be corrected for better relationship.

−SATISH VERMA

New Delhi

09990022287

Contents

Chapter 1

Nasirullah of Mirpur Feels Pain of Leaving His Nation

It was the fourth day of our stay in Mirpur Pakistan. We had reached here by crossing Wagha border. It was a four hours journey from Lahore to Mirpur .I was feeling tired after giving too much time in meeting various people till late night. There was a restlessness inside me and I could not go for sleep. My mind was searching answer of lot of questions. I was totally engulfed in my thoughts. I heard a pious sound of Allah coming from a Mosque- it was a morning Azan. Then I also herd natural morning bell given by a cock family. I came out from my bed and opened the window. The day light was overcoming on the existence of darkness. It was a middle of winter season. I ordered for a cup of tea and switched on T.V.

It was 7'o clock in the morning. Suddenly I received a call from intercom that one old man had come to meet me and was waiting in reception of the hotel. I recalled my memory. Some one Nasirullah Khan had send me a massage. He wanted to meet me. Breaking my thought hotel staff entered into room with tea. A hot tea relaxed me. Then I throw myself into bathroom, after getting fresh and a short prayer to god I made a call on reception and told them to send visitor into my room. I also ordered them to send tea and breakfast for two people.

In next moment, a well built old man was in front of the door of my room. I tried to read him. He was little longer than 6 feet and was carrying blanket of deep colour. He was looking restless and his long beard could not able to hide his emotion.

I welcomed him with folded hand and respectfully took him inside room. I felt a kind of request in his eyes. He started conversation calling me Beta but later used *janab* in entire conversation. This respected old man introduced himself as Nasirullah khan. He was also carrying a bag on his tired shoulder and was trying to pull out some papers out of it. Hotel staff entered with tea and breakfast. I requested Nasirullah khan to have tea & breakfast first. He accepted my request. Nasirullah Khan was dressed with high quality cloth.

After breakfast I straightforward asked him " Chachajan (uncle) what could I do for you" an emotional Nasirullah khan started unfolding himself.

Janab! A lot of people from India had visited here but I found you the most sincere person. I saw you talking with various people with great interest. There I decided to meet you, at least you would listen me.

Thank you Chachajan for giving me respect, now please tell me your reason to come. Because of my gentle words Nasirullah khan felt closer to me and opened his heart telling – Beta (my son) remain aware of the intelligence people, they are moving everywhere and I saw them on reception also. Don't worry Chacha; you say what you want to say. Actually I was very much aware of ISI People and never wanted to kill time in discussing them.

Nasiruallah khan started pouring his hearts in mix language of Gojari and Dogri. His voice was breaking because of out flow of emotion.

My son, now I am at my 75th years of my age. I crossed the border during the 71th war from one of village of Rajouri poonch area, that time I was 45 years old and had heard many good stories about Pakistan but all proved fake and misleading. He continued after taking long breath. We have great freedom in our Kashmir, people can openly speak against government, but here you can not speak a single word. Intelligence people arrest without giving any reason and torture like enemy. Nasirullah's eyes were full of tears. He strongly managed his tears and came on point – Janab I want to fulfill my last wish. Now I am grand father, my parents died but my brother and sister are living in Rajouri (J & K state in india). I want to meet them before I die. Now I am a sick person, if you could do anything then please do it for the sake of Allah.

I felt disturbed and also surprised to see Nasirullah trying to put his pagari on my feet. I stopped him. Nasirullah khan felt sorry and said beta hopes are fading away very fast. When I saw you, found another light of hope. If you people will give your heart and mind, many problem will be solved. You people can convince General Musafraf and Manmohan Singh to help those people who want to return back their homes. Nasirullah could not stop crying like children. I could understand the pain of Nasirullah. I also became emotional and tried hard to console him saying Allah will make everything possible.

Nasirullah had everything in Mirpur but his last wish was to meet his brother & sister who were living in their own nation.

According to Nasirullah, there are big number of people, who had crossed the border during 71th war and before, now want to return back to their roots.

Nasirullah after wiping his tears put a question, what people achieve from war and terrorism? why people don't live with brotherhood and peace ?

Question of Nasirullah deserves to be answered by politicians of both the nations. But probably they don't have answer because they know the reasons behind war and terrorism. I revealed this thought to Nasirullah and said to have faith in Allah (God). God will create a new path someday.

Nasirullah khan, after releasing his emotion said good bye to me but did not forget to say that not to unfold this meeting to anyone otherwise intelligence people would ruin their lives.

A hugely shattered and fearful person Nasirullah khan wanted to meet his brother & sister settled in J & K state in India. Could any one make his last wish possible?

■ ■ ■

Chapter 2

Trying Hard to Break the Ice, Frozen Years Ago

I met with Nasirullah Khan during my second visit of Pakistan. There I got an opportunity to visit Mirpur town situated in Pakistan Occupied Kashmir. This time entire Pakistan was under control of General Parwej Musharraf. He was the supreme power and enough popular around the globe because of his typical style of working.

It is well known fact that history of Indo-Pakistani

PM of India Dr.Manmohan Singh

relationships always remained sour and twisted. India have been taking steps to have better relationship with Pakistan but this time an army General and President of Pakistan had come forward to break the ice, frozen years before. It resulted into a joint statement by Indo-Pak leaders to have regular composite dialogue. This statement was issued on 6th January 2004. It was an occasion of SAARC meeting organized by Pakistan in Islamabad. On this gracious occasion General Parwej Mushraff and Prime Minister of India Atal Bihari Bajpayee had said in a joint statement that terrorism would be rooted out. Though it never happened till now.

Whatever after joint statement, journalists of SAARC Nations first visited India and specially taken to Kashmir. After that journalists of India visited Pakistan. It can be said that both the nation were trying hard to develop a better relationship through SAIFMA (South Asia Free Media Associations) and General Parwej Mushraff had taken this step seriously.

We reached Lahore from Mirpur on 19th November 2004. Here our purpose was to attend two days conference of south Asian journalists. General Parwej Musharff along with other top leaders of Pakistan were supposed to deliver their speech on this occasion.

The then President of Pakistan Parwej Musharraf

For me, it was an opportunity to understand the insight of leaders of Pakistan. I was waiting for that moment anxiously.

A common Indian believes that Pakistan is an enemy state and never be a well wisher of India. In my two visits of Pakistan, I tried to understand the insight of political leaders & political leadership of Pakistan, behavior and motto of Pakistan's army, ISI, Media, various terrorist and fundamentalist organizations and obviously mindset of common citizens. Though it was hard to understand the things with observatory participation within the span of only two weeks, yet I tried my best and utilized every single moment in interacting with maximum number of people. I interacted with intellectuals, army officers, political leaders, fundamentalist, hardcore militants and common citizen of Pakistan. I put my questions & queries to them and tried to sense realities in their answers.

Each and every moment that I spend in Pakistan remained a treasure for me. During Pakistan's visit, I came across such hard facts that completely changed my earlier perceptions. I experienced some of such hard realities during my two visits of Pakistan that I never imagined earlier.

I experienced good, bad and worst experience during both of my visits of Pakistan and all the memories gathered from there are printed on the canvas of my memory and it will remain with me till the last breath of my life.

When you decide to write your memories, the first thing that makes you confuse is where to start? It happened to me also. Memories of both of my visits of Pakistan were equally important. Some of my memories were of political importance and some of were related with history. Some of memories were related to common citizens of Pakistan and some of were very personal experiences of mine but all of memories were wonderful and surprisingly true. Many times I was forced to sink into pages of history and went out to search the related people who remained the part of history. I did all these exercises to know the truth of my memories and experiences of both of Pakistan's visit. Sometimes I had to go in past to calculate authenticity of present. In Pakistan I came across truth, on which Pakistan was being ruled. They pour poison against India in the name of cast, religion and nationality and misguide their own citizens. In the state of Jammu and Kashmir(India), especially in Kashmir, Pakistan's militants display the flag of Pakistan and shout slogans in favour of Pakistan.

In Pakistan I came across political leaders and their political stunts and also experienced truth of militant's organization. All are making fool to common citizen of Pakistan.

I came across the pain and agonies of the citizens of both the nations and how they are suffering because of very poor relationship of both the nations. I am trying to share all my memories, which I cannot forget even I wish.

This book is the outcome of such incidents that is beyond thinking of common Indians....

such truth that generates doubts....

such experiences where life can be saved only with confidence.....

journey of such a place where you can meet death with single mistake...i

Interviewing a person with a question that you decide after hundred of thoughts....

Living with such people where presence of yours itself create tension...

Living such a place where you see death in next step...

Living with such a people, whom credibility is decided on the point of gun or hand grenade...

Such places of worship where you cannot pray for your safety...

Such incidents which can suddenly speed up your pulse...

Such a turns & twists of hill roads where you can hardly breath and have a chance of last breath............
∎∎∎

Chapter 3
Democracy or Dictatorship

This is the memory of my second visit in Pakistan. It was the time when democratic government of Pakistan led by the then Prime-Minister Miyan Nawaj Sharif was overpowered by army of Pakistan and General Parwej Musharraf had appointed himself as president of Pakistan.

The day of 12th October 1999 was very important in the history of Pakistan. It was an evening in Colombo.

Victim of Army Coup, the then Prime Minister of Pakistan Miyan Nawaj Sheriff

General Parwej Musharraf after official tour of Srilanka had taken flight to reach Karanchi. The moment P.K. 805 flight had to land at Karanchi airport, Pakistan air traffic control suddenly took turn and did not give permission to land. Actually the then Prime Minister Miyan Nawaj Shariff had smelled the mind of General Perwej Mushrraf that he could overpower his regime. So he made a plan to suspend him during air journey as General could not react while flying in the air. Pilot was ordered to take flight at the height of 21000 feet and then go outside border of Pakistan.

It was the good luck of General Mushrraf that the moment he knew the plan of Miyan Nawaj Sharif, quickly ordered his two subordinate Generals to immediately cordon the residence of Prime Minister and Pakistan television. Both the subordinate Generals were playing tennis but this order has bigger thrill for them and they implemented it on war basis. Within minutes army took control on Pakistan and allowed flight of General Musharraf to land respectfully. Fuel of flight had reach on dangerous point and few minute late would be disastrous.

It is a world record. Pakistan advocates democracy but Army controlled Pakistan for 48 years in its 62 years of existence.

Army dictator General Ziya Ul Haque(left) who hanged the then Prime Minister Zulfikar Ali Bhutto (right)

An Encounter with Pakistan's Reality

Because of international pressure democracy often prevailed in Pakistan but the Army and ISI always played a bigger role than political leaders. And this face of Pakistan is still continued...

In the international arena it has been proved that democracy cannot run in Pakistan. Army habitually controls the administration and the ISI remains on fore front. Both show their trust more on fundamentalist than common citizens of Pakistan.

The first Prime Minister of Pakistan Likayat Ali Khan was assassinated in 1951 and then his two followers were also killed. In 1979, the most powerful political leader Zulfikar Ali Bhutto was hanged in the military regime of General Ziya Ul haque. These facts were unfolded by the members of Pakistan people's party during an informal conversation. After nine years of Bhutto's capital punishment, Ziya Ul Haque mysteriously died in a plane crash on 17th August 1988. Plane crashed within minutes after taking off from Bahawalpur air track.

In 1971 General Yahyaa Khan was thrown out from power and was confined for five years. It was his luck that he was not ordered to hang.

President Sikandar Mirza and two Prime Ministers of Pakistan, Benazir Bhutto and Miyan Nawaj Sharif was forced to leave Pakistan. Sikandar Mirza and Benezir Bhutto took shelter in London and Nawaj Sharif in Saudi Arab. Benazir Bhutto and Nawaj Sharif were also imprisoned.

Because of international pressure, election was announced in Pakistan and Nawaj sharif and Benajir Bhutto could able to return Pakistan. Later Benazir Bhutto was killed in a blast.

Here I am narrating a popular story about the strength and influence of Pakistan's army.

A Pakistani citizen was travelling in a crowded bus. He felt pressure of an army boot on his feet.

He was feeling pain and hardly could see the man with army boot. With great fear he asked....

Sir are you in the army ?

The man rudely replied " No"

Feeling great pain he asked....

Sir is your father in the army ?

The man again said "No"

In every passing second his pain was becoming unbearable, he collected all his courage and asked....

Sir any member of your family or friend or neighbour work in the army.

The man with great anger shouted " No"

Then go to hell and have your boot on your head. Then, the man threw the Person out of bus.

■ ■ ■

Chapter 4

Beginning of a Memorable Journey

It was just a chance that when I visit Pakistan first time, saw a democratic government headed by Prime-Minister, Miyan Nawaj Sharif. The then Prime-minister of India Atal Bihari Bajpayee and government of Pakistan both were trying hard to achieve a better relationship. Both the nations were putting their efforts to lessen bitterness in their relationship. Delhi-Lahore Bus service was started to spread the message of

Atal Behari Bajpayee

brotherhood in between citizens of both the nations. I got an opportunity to be a part of those journalists who were selected to visit Pakistan by Delhi-Lahore Bus Service.

When I visit Pakistan second time, General Musharraf was the president of Pakistan. Pakistan based terrorist organizations had attacked on Indian parliament and it resulted into worst relationship between the two nations.

On the basis of facts, India reached on conclusion that the ISI was involve in the terrorist attack on Indian parliament.

We reached Pakistan in tense situation. There we closely saw the difference between administration of a democratic government and an army rule. I became witness of the devastating lives of common citizen of Pakistan. Earlier I was listening about their worst condition this time I was experiencing being a part of them.

A conference was organized on 20 & 21th November 2004 in Lahore through SAFMA and the subject was "world of news & interaction with each other". All the journalists & intellectuals were trying hard to establish peace in South Asia region through proper interaction and discussion. India had taken initiative and first SAFMA conference was organized in India where selected journalist from Pakistan had come to participate. 19tn selected Pakistani journalist was taken to India`s Jammu & Kashmir. It was expected from them that they would see the ground reality of Jammu & Kashmir and would write positive to give a boost to peace process.

A scene of Bagha Border

It was also believed that journalists from Pakistan would go Pakistan Occupied Kashmir and narrate them the real face of Jammu and Kashmir that was far different than their propaganda. During this period it was decided that selected Indian journalists who have expertise

An Encounter with Pakistan's Reality

on Kashmir issue will visit Pakistan to attain conference on Indo-Pakistani relationship. It was also decided that 20 journalists specially from India's Jammu and Kashmir who write on Kashmir issue will also attain SAFMA Conference at Lahore. Journalists were also supposed to be taken to Azad Jammu and Kashmir. I was one amongst 20 journalists who were selected from India's Jammu and Kashmir.

It was going to be my second visit to Pakistan and I was really excited. I was sure that this visit would be more memorable and more exciting than previous one. This time we were going to see an Army rule in Pakistan.

A talk was in air that this time Indian journalists will get opportunity to see those territory of Pakistan Occupied Kashmir and Pakistan for which they don't issue visa.

All the selected Indian journalist had to assemble at Delhi. I also joined in the wagon. From Delhi we all reached Amritsar by train, then we were taken to Wagha border. This Wagha border is famous around the globe as tourist place.

Hotal Avari of Lahore where the SAFMA conference was organised

Every evening army of both side participate in flag hosting ceremony and people from all corner come here to see this function.

According to Indian time Wagha border remains open from 10 am to 4 pm for those who cross the border with valid visa. For we journalists government of Pakistan had arranged a luxury bus to carry us from Wagha border.

After completing the formality, we took seat in bus and within 30 minutes of time reached Lahore. Conference was organized in an international hotel named AAWARI, situated in the middle of the city Lahore.

We reached Hotel Aawari in evening and were welcomed by State Minister of Art, Culture & Sports Janab Mohammad Ali Durrani. Here I must say that till reaching the Lahore, I never felt it was an another nation. I felt moving in an another state of our Nation.

We had to complete formality of registration to participate in conference. This formality took time. We Indian journalist started meeting one another and also with local journalists during the process of registration. Now it became night. We all became part of group dinner which was nicely arranged. After dinner we came out from the hotel to have fresh air and to feel the ecstasy of being in Pakistan. We interacted with local people and tried to understand the internal situation of Pakistan. 19th October 2004 had slipped from hand and now it was midnight. My heart was forcing me to walk on the roads of Pakistan but we had to live there with certain limitations. I had to sleep because next morning was going to be the most busy day.

■ ■ ■

Chapter 5
Jammu and Kashmir Issue Rules the Seminar

It was 20th November 2004. We were supposed to get ready early in the morning. We hardly had the time for tea & breakfast in hotel and so, we went out to do various activities related to the conference. Local representatives and coordinators had filled up the place before time. General Parwej Musharaf was supposed to inaugurate the conference. I was anxiously waiting for this historical moment.

General Secretary of SAFMA Imtiyaz Alam with author Satish Verma at Sammelan Venue

Conference started with the welcome speech of M.Ziauddin, the secretary of SAFMA of Pakistan's branch, then General Perwej Mushrraf formally inaugurated the conference. Then, the General secretary of SAFMA Janab Imityaz Aalam, delivered his speech describing the need and motto of SAFMA conference.

We all were desperate to listen speech of General Parwej Mushhrraf; and I was sure General will discuss Kashmir.

General Mushrraf came an dias, started his speech and said "all the violent incidents of Kashmir is the outcome of freedom movement of Kashmiri people. Unless and until problem of Kashmir will be sorted out , movement inside Kashmir cannot be stopped.

General strongly advocated that people of Kashmir have seen enough blood bath and now want to achieve peaceful solution.

General became diplomatic and said " India's step to curtail the number of army in valley is a welcome step but it may be a part of diplomacy.

General further detailed his meeting with Prime-minister Manmohan Singh in New York. Both had issued a joint statement but nothing could be achieved till today on this issue.

General mushrraf was trying hard to convince us that Kashmir is national issue for the people of Pakistan and must be sorted out earliest giving full attention. General though did not open but said he had many formulas to sort out conflict of Kashmir.

In his 40minutes speech, General did not speak a single word about the media. He stuck to the Kashmir issue only. He repeatedly argued that Pakistan feels closer to Afghanistan and Kashmir. Kashmir must get such solution as is acceptable to India, Pakistan and the people of

Kashmir. General also made a controversial statement that the "All Party Hurriyat Conference" of Kashmir is the real representative of people of Kashmir.

General also focused on the problem of terrorism in Pakistan and strongly said that Govt. of Pakistan was very much capable to handle foreign terrorists.

Further General throws a satire that Delhi-Lahore bus service can not fetch any solution. Yes SAFMA could be a bridge to create an environment for the beginning of new Indo-Pak relationship.

Then, Governor of Punjab state of Pakistan & former Lieutenant General (Khalid Maqbul Elahi) were present on this occasion. K.K.Katyal, the SAFMA secretary of Indian branch and General Secretary Vinod Sharma were also present on dias.

One interesting thing happened there. The venue of lunch was changed from hotel to governor's house of Punjab state; and it was the decision of General Parwej Musharraf. It was decided that General will interact with journalists from Jammu and Kashmir during lunch period and will answer their queries. Actually it had been done on the request of journalist from Jammu & Kashmir.

I got an opportunity to interact with General Parwej Musharraf.

Actually General had given two different statements on two different occasions to solve Kashmir problem. In one statement,he had said that undivided Kashmir should be divided into seven parts and in his second statement, he had insisted on polling on Kashmir issue and added that what the people of Kashmir wanted could be the solution. I asked him, what would be the best solution to solve Kashmir issue.

This question put all of them in a state of shock. For

some moments General maintained silence and then, he answered with trembling voice. I did not get any satisfaction with his answer. After question- answer session, we all were assembled for afternoon meal. General Musharraf was looking relaxed. A light situation was present. Indian Film Veer-Zara was running in some cinema halls in Pakistan and people were appreciating this film. To make the situation light General started talking about this film. Though general had not seen this movie, he had heard a lot about it. Suddenly, changing his tone, General complained that whenever Indian film makers made film on Indo-Pakistani subject, or a love story, they always showed girl from Pakistan. Why? I did not hesitate in answering his question with due apology. I said, "Sir , actually for making a love story, film makers search an innocent and bubbly girl and they find these qualities in Pakistani girl, they are no less than Indian girls."

Author along with General Parwej Musharraf and Secretary of Press Club Manu Srivats at Punjab State Governor's House in Pakistan

My answer created a silence for a while but in next moment, all smiled including the General. But General had a lot of complaints with Indian film makers. He said, " An average and weak Indian hero fights with hundreds of strong fighters and he defeats our army, seems all nonsense". I understood that General must had seen some such Indian movies where Indian hero defeats army of Pakistan. We returned to our hotel to attained next session of conference. We had a discussion on the reedom of press after 9/11 attack. Christopher warne(from world editors forum) Dr. Havrad (the secretary of IFJ) and other top journalists addressed in second session of the seminar.

After evening tea & breakfast, a special program titled, " Meeting with understanding" was scheduled . Prime-Minister of Pakistan Shaukat Aziz had come to preside over the evening program. Entire day gone like fast blowing wind. The Venue of night meal again had to be changed again from hotel to the government residence of former Lieutenant General ,Khalid Maqbul Sahab. We all were discussing Jammu and Kashmir during the night meal. Later, honourable Governor honored all journalists from Jammu and Kashmir with momentoes. That way, one more day was passed.

■ ■ ■

Chapter 6

Jammu and Kashmir Issue Fired Again

Though we don't had any doubt on the President General Parwej Musharraf regarding his honest effort to make better Indo-Pakistani relationship yet we were sure that Kashmir issue would play major role in this seminar.

It was the second day of seminar and many known & famous personalities of Pakistan were scheduled to address. Everything was happening according to schedule.

I ever had a thought in mind that from Guru Nanak to Sufi saint Bulle Shah, Sufi singer Ghulam Ali, Nurshat Fateh Ali khan, Abida Parveen....all Pakistani saints and artists have taught love, spread brotherhood and sang songs of unity and integrity, then why Pakistan never show the character according to its great legacy. Why India and Pakistan, who are like two brothers, cannot have good relationship. It seems that some unseen negative force have cursed the land of Pakistan and put fundamentalism and terrorism into it to face one after another hell and to have unending fight with India. A Pakistani citizen Md.Ilyas had blamed America for playing the role of villain in-between India & Pakistan. It is notable that common citizen of both the nations always remain ready to welcome each-other with open arms.

21 November 2004, second day of seminar. Foreign Minister of Pakistan Khurshid Mahmood Kasuri were chief guest. He delivered his speech focusing mainly on Kashmir. He said conditional peace could not be accepted. Mr. Khurshid also cleared that Pakistan have better relationship with America and it must not be concluded that this Indo-Pakistani peace process have been organized under any pressure of America. Foreign Minister also showed his anger. According to him it was difficult to forget past but still they were working hard to achieve peace for better future.

He appreciated Indian media for playing great role in Indian democracy.

Mr. Kasuri also said that in last 57years, neither India nor Pakistan could achieve success in developing better relationship between them, though General Musharraf put all his efforts to develop better relationship with India and the best example could be seen in his Agra visit. He also said that Delhi-Lahore bus service could bear fruitful result. To participate in this conference few fundamentalist leaders were also invited and some of them were given chance to speak from dais.

It prooved the strong relationship between army rule and fundamentalist organizations.

Fundamentalist leaders like Mushahid Hussian, General secretary of Pakistan Muslim league, Liyakat Bluch of Punjab state, were present in seminar and got opportunity to address the press fraternity assembled in SAFMA Conference.

One of leader of opposition Maulana Fazallur Rahman dramatically said that " Ab Baat Goli Se Nahin Boli Se Banegi"

(Now the problem will be solved with dialogues not guns)

When we request him to speak on J and K issue, he gently denied. One thing was very much clear. All the Pakistanis either Army personnel, or political leader, or media person or intellectuals whoever got opportunity to speak form dais, all raised the issue of Kashmir.

It become clear for us that issues like poverty, unemployment, drugs, smuggling, worst economy of Pakistan had no meaning in front of Kashmir issue.

I realized that even common Pakistani citizens don't forget to add Kashmir issue in their conversation.

I can recall the speech of Zulfikar ALi Bhutto during 1965 Indo-Pak war. He had said, If India makes nuclear Bomb, we will also make. We will eat grass, will fill our stomach with leaves or will remain empty stomach but will make nuclear bomb.

On 18 may 1974, India exploded its first nuclear device named operation Smiling Buddha. And then on 11 and 13 may 1988 India conducted explosion of five nuclear devices. Following India's nuclear program, 0n 28 & 30th may 1988 Pakistan exploded series of nuclear devices and became a first Muslim Nation with nuclear power.

Whatever all the news papers of Pakistan and Pakistan television were covering this seminar. It was all biased journalism. The political party in power MMA including all the opposition leaders of Pakistan looked serious for a dialogue with India to achieve peace in Kashmir. And this face of Pakistan leaders had been continuously projected through Pakistani media.

During this seminar, one of journalist from Kashmir raised an issue that kashmiri journalist don't get right treatment in India. It made all of us surprised and we all felt shame. It was hard to digest this stupid statement. Actually some of Kashmir journalists tried to create an environment against India with false and baseless allegations.

They even said that Kashmiri journalist were forced to keep silence and face false F.I.R. & Court cases. It was very much clear that some big power had influenced to those Kashmiri journalist who had put allegations.

It is an obvious fact that Indian journalist enjoy total freedom in India and India has complete freedom of press.

Freedom of Press in India is unmatchable. Probably our few Kashmiri journalist were misled by some fundamentalist organizations of Pakistan and the ISI. The ISI was trying hard to influence some Indians to be used against India. We all journalist from India were shocked with this incident. At last Vinod sharma, political editor of Times of India had to come forward to prove that allegations were baseless & fabricated. Vinod sharma gave a strong example narrating arrest of a Kashmiri journalist Iftikhar Gilani because of doubt. Security people had collected some objectionable documents from him. Then Indian journalist association had started a campaign for the release of Kashmiri journalist Iftikhar Gilani. Though it was an open fact that Iftikhar Gilani was the Son-in-law of Kashmiri separatist leader Syed Ali Shah Gilani. The statement of Vinod Sharma helped a lot in releasing tension that was erupted with wrong reasons.

In this seminar Kashmiri journalists were getting more attention. Their interviews were being telecast on Pakistan television without any censor & cut, even in news papers they were getting bigger space.

It came to an end of 21th Nov. 2004. It remained a busy day. We became part of an entertainment program at night. It was organized by Ministry of Art & Literature and Chief Minister of Punjab Choudhary Parwej Elahi presided over

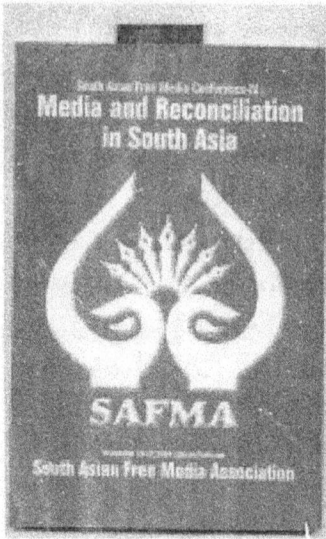

South Asian Free Media Conference-II
Media and Reconciliation in South Asia

SAFMA

South Asian Free Media Association

army rule has become

the function. It was almost impossible to interact with outside people because of the busy schedule. I was thinking, it might be a plan of Government of Pakistan to kept us busy.. It was an obvious fact that the ISI had an open eye on all of us and on all of our activities. Earlier my Pakistani friend had informed me regarding these fact. And it was quite natural in the country like Pakistan where the ISI dominated every sphere and

■■■

Chapter 7

Wonderful Lahore

It was 22nd November 2004, early morning. we were getting ready to see Lahore. Lahore carries soul of Pakistan. If you visit Pakistan and don't see Lahore, then you just have wasted your tour.

Lahore is a city situated in the state of Punjab in Pakistan. It is a beautiful city with great historical and cultural importance. Lahore has maintained its historical magic even after modern changeover.

Famous Urdu Poet Jauk has written about the streets of old Delhi – "Kaun jaye jauk ye delli ki galiyan chhorkar" (Nobody could leave streets of Delhi.)

People say about Kashmir that if heaven exists anywhere on the earth then it is Kashmir, Kashmir and kashmir......and in the same way people say about Lahore that if you have not seen Lahore, you have seen nothing.(Jinha Lahore nahin vekhya, onha kuchh nahin vekhya)

Before partition of India Lahore was identified as a city of Art & Culture and even after partition it is known as cultural city of Pakistan.

City Lahore also has become important centre of business in Pakistan. But all its greatness have come under the shadow of terrorism.

From 10 a.m to 1.30 p.m was the scheduled time for the movement. These three and half hour was very short time to see the city Lahore.

I knew that even a complete month is not sufficient time to see the city Lahore completely. It was my good luck that I had an earlier opportunity to stay at Lahore for four days and had seen Lahore with more time in hand.

What I saw in Lahore, will give you detail when I will write memories of my first visit to Pakistan. Though I had gone through some bitter experiences that still haunts me. I cannot forget the incident when at Mall Road; a famous road of city Lahore, ISI (Pakistani intelligence agency) tried to abduct me. It was a long incidence and I will narrate it in detail in my next book. This time I was with a team and was feeling the difference. We had been given map of Lahore from tourist point of view by Tourism information centre of Pakistan. This map had all the important information about Lahore written in English & Urdu.

For me to move on the roads of Lahore was just like seeing a photograph repeatedly. We stopped at Gurudwara. It was a replica of any other Gurudwara of India in terms of look & management. Here I must say that a place of worship always gives peace of mind and lead towards ecstasy. Temple, Mosque, Gurudwara or Church, all are places of worship and have equal importance for the humanity at large. But Pakistan has been erected on the foundation of religion and religion plays greater role in running of the administration of the nation. Existence of other religion and religious structures in Pakistan is not accepted with open heart. But here in this Gurudwara we found a strange thing, a former Muslim ISI officer was appointed to look after this Gurudwara. I simply said , Great !

An Encounter with Pakistan's Reality

For afternoon meal we were invited by District mayor Miyan Aamir Mahmood and the venue was Jinnah Garden.

Though conference of SAFMA had come to an end, yet some formalities were left to complete. After afternoon meal, we were taken back to Aawari Hotel. All were meeting one another thinking will meet again in India. I was also trying to meet maximum number of people to make some new relationship.

■■■

Chapter 8
Fundamentalist Leader:
Maulana Fazalurrahman

I remained busy in writing special report on SAFMA Sammelan for our National news paper **Rastriya Sahara**. Actually I wanted to summaries entire conference incorporating my experience in one big article.

Fundamentalist leader of Pakistan Maulana Fazalurrahman

An Encounter with Pakistan's Reality

All the Pakistani who were either in power or in opposition or belonged to an intellectual class, were advocating a continuous Indo-Pak peace process to solve Kashmir problem. I found editorials of most of the News Papers of Pakistan, filled with warning for India. But surprisingly I found one of famous fundamentalist and religious leader Maulana Fazalrrahman liberal and soft.

Though he was also taking about Indo-Pakistani dialogues to achieve peace but at the same time criticizing earlier Pakistan Governments for their wrong decision. Straight forward he said that for a time period Pakistan had reached on dead end because of Kargir War. Maulana Fazalurrahman went one step further telling that Kargil War had made Pakistan answerable.

He openly criticized the then Prime-Minister of Pakistan Nawaj Sharif for mishandling the whole Kargil incidence. In one hand he was talking about peace with India and on the other hand put entire Pakistani Army into Kargil War. I was surprised that Fazalurrahan did not take name of General Parwej Musharraf, though he was Army Chief of Pakista during Kargil War. General Parwej has briefly written in his autobiography "The Line of fire" that he would not be blamed for Kargil war. Very diplomatically he put all the illegations on India for Kargil War. General willfully adopted a policy to defame India and tried hard to prove himself innocent.

General has mentioned a fake story in his autobiography. He writes: - "India claimed to destroy two attacks by Pakistan Army on them in the glacier region on 16 & 17th October 1988.

Generla further writes : " My officer never attacked on them. I also tried to know from the officer of Northern Command area and all to them said no for any kind of attack from Pakistan 's side.

At the end of October, I was reported about five attacks by Indian army.

According to the statement of General, Army of Pakistan never raid or intruded in Indian territory.

Further General writes - "Later he came to know that Kashmiri Mujahiddin were involve in all the raid and most of them were the citizen of India`s Kashmir . Indian raiders with help of Mujahhiddins supported by Pakistan used to cross line of control now and often from difficult passages. You can understand the game being played by Army of Pakistan and the ISI.These words clearly shows the foul play of Pakistan and foul mind set of General Parwej Musharraf. General has mentioned one more incidence. He intensely went into intelligence report send by Rawalpindi Kot Army Headquarter. According to this report, India have been blaming on Pakistan for various attacks. The then Defence Minister of India George Fernandis were frequently visiting in Kargil region and it all showed the intension of India to fight with Pakistan.

The most surprising element that General has revealed through his autobiography is that the Army of Pakistan has been fighting jointly with Mujahhiddins. Army of Pakistan has been continuously helping Mujahhiddins. Because of this reason Mujahhiddin could able to capture 800sq. kilometers land from India. Further General has described that those 800 sq. kilometers land were of Mashko, Drass, Kaksur, Baltic & Shyok region.

I was talking about Fazalurrahman . He was talking like real saint. He said that disintegration of soviet Russia and 9/11 attack on America have changed the global thought. The whole world is passing through geographical and political change and it has also changed the thought of India & Pakistan. Now both the nations want to achieve peaceful relationship through peaceful dialogues. Though Issue of

Kashmir has become national issue of Pakistan .

Maulana wanted to come out with such a solution that was acceptable to the Government of India , Pakistan and also to the people of Kashmir. So People of Kashmir must remain part of every dialogues between the two nations. Fazalurrahman also narrated about his India visit during the reign of Prime Minister Atal Bihari Bajpai and appreciated the efforts that had been taken during his tenure to solve the Kashmir issue. But later Congress came in power in India and they did not show the will to solve the Kashmir problem. At the end Maulana showed his hope on Prime minister Manmohan Singh that he would try his best to have stable solution of Kashmir problem.

Maulana Fazalurrahman had shown his liberal face, but the other fundamentalist leaders like Meer Kazi Hussain of Jamate-Islami showed his hard-core face on Kashmir problem. He even blamed that Government of General Musharraf already had a deal with the Government of India.

■■■

Chapter 9

Self-praised Army of Pakistan

From Lahore we had to move towards Pakistan occupied Kashmir to see Mirpur, situated in Kotli region. Here I want to unfold a fact that Government of Pakistan and officers of the Pakistan Army never accept their defeat in the hands of India in 1971 Indo-Pakistani War. They mislead the common citizens of Pakistan with false and negative propaganda. I saw a fighter plane of India which was crashed in the territory of Pakistan during 1971 Indo-Pakistani war, displayed near ShishMahal Chowk of Anarkali market in Lahore. For Pakistanis at Large, it was a symbol of bravery of the army of Pakistan. I saw self-praised words were written on it in bold letters. They never accept that Pakistani Army had surrendered in front of Indian army   after humiliating defeat. Even after facing deep economical trouble, Pakistan remained adamant to take revenge from India for its 1971 defeat in Indo-Pakistani war. Actually Pakistan has developed a strong enemy status with India and has been behaving like enemy nation.

They have made a highway connecting Lahore to capital city Islamabad in such a way that it could be utilized as air runway in emergency . They are living with vision to have a great war with India. Here is an another example that shows how deeply Pakistan has been nourishing its vision to have a war with India. Pakistan started its nuclear program neglecting the protest of international community and became nuclear power. Now people of Pakistan feel proud to have such an achievement. In international arena Pakistan is being treated as Islamic Bomb, and Pakistan never accepts this identity. Rulers of Pakistan put few questions......

" Why America and Europe are not called Christian Bomb?

Why India is not called a Hindu Bomb?

Why international community holds double standards and projects Pakistan's nuclear power as Islamic Power ?

Here is one more example of self praised bravery of Pakistan. We Indians celebrates Kargil War as Vijay Diwas (Day of victory) and Pakistan also projects themselves winner of Kargil War. Gereral Parwej Musharraf in his autobiography has dramatically clarified that how Pakistan is winner of Kargil War. In Kargil War 200 Pakistani jawans (Soldiers) were killed and 415 were wounded. But India claimed to have loss the lives of 600 jawan and 1500 jawans were wounded. General Parwej Musharraf further writes: " the actual numbers of Indian soldiers killed by Pakistani army are double than projected by India and it has been proved with coffin scam of India. The Army of Pakistan is far greater and powerful than Indian army is a proven fact".

At one place General has written that India almost gone weird to celebrate Kargil War as their biggest victory and in the process they announced greatest bravery award to martyr of Kargil War. Later it came to know that one of posthumously awarded soldier was alive.

Here it is important to reveal that Pakistan projects everything in the light of Islam and under the influence of Islamic fundamentalist leaders. But one thing surprised me. We had given a map by tourism department of Paksitan to know the Lahore city better. From the written worldon this map, we came to know that Lahore was established 4000 years ago by LAV, son of the Hindu God Almighty Ram. Lahore was named on the name of LAV. God Ram had two sons named LAV and KUSH. If one city was established by LAV then there must be some other city established by KUSH also. My curiosity was satisfied when I came to know that KUSH had established a village "Kushak". When we travel from Wagha border to Lahore, Kushak comes in the way.

Entire days remained busy. We enjoyed night meal at the residence of Janab Shahid Rafi, the then secretary of Information & Broadcasting Ministry of Pakistan. Night meal was followed with melodious musical program.

Editor of magzine Organizer, Tarun Vijay was present there. 22nd November 2004 flew away like fast blowing wind.

The morning of 23rd November 2004: It was a Good-Bye ceremony for all the representatives of SAFMA SAMMELAN.

Some of selected journalist had to move to visit Mirpur, in kotli region of Pakistan Occupied Kashmir. I was also one of them. I was excited to see Mirpur and entire kotli region. It was hard to get visa for this part of Pakistan Occupied Kashmir and I was getting an opportunity to visit there. I was expecting this visit more exciting than earlier one. I must tell you that this part of Pakistan Occupied Kashmir mesmerizes with its natural beauty and on the other hand terrorist training camps and launching pads closer to line of control create terror.

■■■

Chapter 10

Escape from an Abduction in Lahore

Already I have given a picture of Lahore in Chapter " Wonderful Lahore". Again I say Lahore is wonderful. Lahore a cultural center of Pakistan, has more importance for me. It remained a land of work and worship for my Parents, and thus I ever feel emotionally attached with the city of Lahore.

Mal Road of Lahore, here author just escaped from an abduction

My Late father and my mother had joined Quit India Movement on the call of Mahatma Gandhi and in the leadership of Sardar Lahana Singh in Lahore. And see the irony I visited Pakistan as a citizen of another Nation. I first visited Pakistan during the tenure of Prime - Minister Nawaj Sherif. A special Delhi-Lahore Bus Service was started to lessen the bitterness in the Indo-Pak relationship. The then Prime - Minister of India Atal Bihari Bajpayee had shown great interest in the opening of Delhi-Lahore Bus service. I got an opportunity to be a part of a team of Media Person who were invited to attain SAFMA SAMMELAN organized by Pakistan. A big team of Indian Journalists became witness of Delhi-Lahore bus service.

Whenever some one visits India from Pakistan or Pakistan from India, feels danger of ISI. I also faced the heat of ISI & had miraculous escape. In Lahore, I got accommodation in a local hotel. There I found sending a fax was too costly and it forced me to go GPO(General Post Office) every day to fax an article to be published in Rastriya Sahara News Paper in India. Like everyday's routine, I wrote story and took a Auto Rikshaw to reach GPO from hotel. The Auto was running on mal road and I was about to reach GPO. Suddenly three motorist tried to stop my Auto. Pathan Auto driver looked towards me and asked what he would do ? I said him to take side and stop. All three motorist were in civil dress, they cornered me and introduced themselves as officers of ISI. I was shocked to see them. I was a citizen of their enemy Nation. They asked stupid questions, checked my visa and passport. One thing that helped me, was my language. I started talking in Punjabi. Within few seconds, local crowd gathered there and supported me thinking a citizen of Pakistan. I also had long beard. Seeing support of local people , One of motorist suddenly took turn and said it was their duty and all three went away. I felt relieved and took long breath. One of local said to me brother God have saved you otherwise they could have taken you at some unknown place and what happened there with you, only God could know ? Later I came to know from local people that intelligence people had cornered my Auto with the intension to abduct me. They could do anything & anywhere.

I thanked God and sit inside auto, Pathan driver started auto and it was again running on the mall road. Driver asked me "Janab, whatever happened with you, could happen with a Pakistani in India. Could CID of India dare to arrest anyone by cornering anywhere in India. God has just saved you". He stopped auto at the gate of GPO, I paid Auto fair and walked towards fax counter. I saw a long queue there. I was puzzled with the incidence happened with me on Mal road and here long queue puzzled me more. I asked the reason for long queue to one of staff at GPO, he replied in loud voice that FAX machine got technical fault and was not working. People in queue reacted in their own way and leave the GPO immediately. I was still there with a confused mind. The staff who had announced that Fax machine was not working, tried to judge me from top to bottom and then said to me - " should I tell you in more laud voice that fax machine is not working". I came out from my thought and interacted with him telling that I was an Indian Journalist and had to send a report through fax to be published in National News Paper in India. Actually I was at Lahore to cover Lahore-Delhi Bus service.My words created an impact on GPO staff and suddenly he changed his attitude. With due respect he said to me " Janab you have come from India then certainly I will try my best to rectify the fault in fax machine." The GPO staff entered into his cabin and in next moment came out showing his great happiness. He said " Janab God is great, fax machine automatically started functioning". He took pages of my article and send it through fax. One thing that I experienced there was the attitude of Government employee. It was almost similar in both the nations. If mood is not right, just announce that system is not working. Whatever when I was returning from GPO, the GPO staff wanted to know that would I visit GPO tomorrow also or not - I said yes. Here I must mention that GPO staff helped me after knowing that I was an Indian. It revealed that common citizens of both the nations don't hate one-another.

Next day I again reached GPO. The same GPO staff was on fax counter. He saw me and ordered in loud voice for two cup of tea. He requested me to have a cup of tea with him if not in hurry. I accepted his offer and found my acceptance made him really cheerful. We started talking with the sip of tea. The GPO staff talked about Taj Mahal, Pious Dargah Of Ajmer Sharif, Sachin Tendulkar and other many things. During conversation he became emotionally charged. He said " Janab you the people are so good then why both the Nations fight each-other. War between both the nations shatter only common citizens. War comes with disaster. Big people play politics and common people die. He put a very common question to me that must had come directly from his heart " Will it ever be possible that both the nations will have good relationship, and will interact with love and brotherhood. Citizens of both the nations will feel free to come and go in either nations and possibly will also able to do business.Sir, believe me, if India & Pakistan will become a friendly nation, the rest of the world will salute us". I was also getting emotionally charged. I said him " Janab I am getting late". He took my papers immediately and send it through fax. I was returning back to hotel but my mind was filled with the thoughts of a common Pakistani. I realized and experienced the real peace and brotherhood in-between common people of both the Nations. Might someday top political leaders will understand it.

■■■

Chapter 11
America and China Are Villains

Pakistani was born with the division of India and still carries unmatchable quality of welcoming its guests. You will find everything beautiful in Pakistan. But it is a matter of surprise, that the land of Pakistani is being abused and hammered with extreme of violence. War and terrorism have affected new generation very badly and questions everybody that what they are giving in the hands of new generation, books or guns. Violence and terrorism kill the people. With these methods one can kill the people or terrorize them but cannot win their hearts. Suppose they kill all the people, then on whom they will rule. If all the water pot will be destroyed then from where common people will drink water. India have emerged as the most powerful nation in South Asia and deserve to be protected for the benefit of entire South Asia, but few fundamentalists and terrorist organizations are involve in blasting and mercilessly killing of innocent people. They are killing

Night Food Market at Lahore

humanity. Their acts can not be justified on any ground. No any religion or book allows anyone to adopt violence to achieve right or wrong target. Violence itself is a sin. Owner or Dhaba (Road side restaurant) had break my thought, my food was served on table. Actually I was in famous Night Food Market at Lahore. I ate there and returned back to my hotel. It was my first visit in Pakistaniistan and I had to know and understand a lot of things. I had a visa for limited period so I had limited time to know various faces of Pakistan.

Next day I along with two other Indian journalist friend reached the famous Government College of Lahore. There we interacted with professor and students of history and political science. It was an interesting meeting. All were

Shah- e- Minar of Lahore

serious in discussing impact of partition on economic growth, religion and Kashmir issue. Students of Political Science, both boys and girls shed their emotions openly on Kashmir problem, But they also realized that bitter relationship between both the countries have resulted into wars, terrorism, loss of man power and loss of economy and trust. Terrorism and wars have ruined the scope of mutual peace and hammered hard to the common people of both the Nations. Both India & Pakistan got independence same night but India has developed with commendable speed and left Pakistan far behind. Students also realized that Pakistan is being trapped in the net of China and America. Pakistani don't have it own policy which can lead the nation towards development. Pakistan must have its own strong policy to follow. Students were practical at thought but during the discussion on Kashmir problem, all became emotional and appeal to the leaders of both the nations to have permanent peace earliest.

During discussion on religion one of professor revealed that modern generation with rich family background don't get time to read and understand religion. They are imitating western culture and it has become a matter of big concern. During three and half hour stay at college campus we also discussed Allama-e-Ikbal, who has written "SAARE JAHAN SE ACHHA HINDUSTAN HAMARA." I must mention here that all the professors and students accepted us just after listening a one line introduction that we are journalist from India. Their welcome and respect will remain forever with us.

After achieving great satisfaction in the association of students and professors at Government College we moved towards famous Anaarkali Market. From cloth to shoe, make-up articles, Afghani shawls, round caps and other hundreds of things one could buy here. We took some light food in a restaurant and walk around the market. Personally I wanted to buy many items but pocket hardly allowed to buy a handmade beautifully designed shawl for my Mother. We returned back to hotel. Now we had only one day left to stay in Pakistan.

Next morning, after breakfast ,I along with a Pakistani journalist friend reached Lahore Fort by car. Here we saw a Gurudwara and bow down our heads in front of Takht. Then took a walk towards fort. There I read a scripture written on the gate of the fort. According to this scripture, The City Lahore was established by LAV, Son of Lord Ram. Inside fort we found sculptures of elephant at many places and Sun was designed on the roof. These are Hindu symbols and reflect that City Lahore was constructed by a Hindu King.

In Pakistan City Rawalpindi is known as an Army Cantonment area, City Karachi is a business center and a port of Pakistan, and Islamabad is a center of political activities. On 23 March 1940, Muslim league of India had passed a bill to form an independent & new Nation Pakistan. In the memory of that Bill Government of Pakistani and erected a Minar of 60 feet high and named " Minar-e-Pakistani". Massages from Kuran has been written in one side of the Minar and on the other side some lines has been imprinted in the honor of Father of the Nation Mohammed Ali Jinnah and great author, Philosopher, Poet and thinker Allma-e-Ikbal.

As we see captured Pakistani tanks displaced at various cities and in some Army Cantonments, to reflect the bravery of Indian army, in the same fashion, an Indian fighter plane which was crashed in the territory of Pakistan during 1971 Indo-Pakistani war has been displayed on the main chowk of Lahore to reflect the bravery of Pakistani army.

An Encounter with Pakistan's Reality

Gurudwara Nankana Sahib is situated in the north-west of Lahore at the distance of 75 kilometer. This is the most pious place for the entire Sikh Community because this place is the birth place of Guru Nanak Dev, the founder of Sikh Religion. He was born there on 1469. Lahore is such a city where a Hindustani can easily feel living in one of city in India. There is a complete Indianisation one can feel in the behavior, look and structure of Lahore.

If you have come as tourist then you can be stopped anywhere in Lahore. You can be asked to show your passport and visa, you can be searched and you can be forced to give bribe and at last you can find yourself cheated by a fake police. One more thing that really attracts attention of onlookers on the roads of Lahore, is the beautifully decorated trucks, buses, autos and other vehicles. Decorated vehicles give different look and identity to the roads of Lahore. Walking on the roads of Lahore gives a different feeling than moving any where in the Pakistan. Lahore has a magic and captures your attention. When you leave Lahore, it calls you back. Lahore is wonderful and touches your soul.

But few things have defamed Lahore as a city and Pakistan as a Nation. Militants, fundamentalists and terrorist organizations like Jamat-ul-Dawa, Lashkar-e-Taiba etc have opened their offices in Lahore. They are a bigger threat not only for India but also for Pakistan. These organizations openly work against India, spread violence and even collect donations for armed struggle in Kashmir. Those militant organizations have become very powerful in Pakistan. They even dare to demonstrate violence on every good occasion. They had even demonstrated against arrival of the PM of India Atal Bihari Bajpayee at Lahore during opening ceremony of Delhi-Lahore Bus Service. They are against any kind of Indo-Pakistani friendship.
■■■

Chapter 12

Home of Terrorists: Azad Jammu & Kashmir

After offering Johar ki Namaj (afternoon prayer at Mosque) we all had a lunch and then sit in a mini bus to move towards our destination. As I discussed earlier that it was almost impossible to had visa to visit Pakistan Occupied Kashmir, but this time it became possible because of General Parwej Musharraf. Probably he wanted to enhance his image and offered Indian journalist to see entire kotli region and Mirpur of Pakistan Occupied Kashmir. Whatever we were grateful to General for providing us this great opportunity.

It was a winter season. Our mini bus were passing through foggy weather. We were escorted by Pakistani rangers , who were running ahead of us in Army Jeep equipped with hooter sound. We were travelling with cold wind and an excitement together. Before Partition Mirpur was a Hindu dominated area and undivided Jammu and Kashmir was being ruled by Dogra ruler. Now it is under the administration of Pakistan. I have gone through a lot of stories about Mirpur. We have a Mirpur road in Jammu connecting Jammu Medical college to Bakshi Nagar. A good number of migrated people from Mirpur live here. They are called Mirpuriya.

An Encounter with Pakistan's Reality

Soon day light was overpowered by darkness because of fog and cold weather. We had to cover a distance of 225 kilometers from Lahore to Mirpur. Our mini bus crossed Ravi Bridge and then stopped on Lala Musaji G.T. Road near a road side tea stall. We took tea and felt fresh. When owner of tea stall knew about us that we belonged to India's Jammu and Kashmir, he felt rejuvenated. He started pouring his queries "Janab I have heard that your Jammu and Kashmir is heaven on Earth."

I replied in yes and also admired him and his Kashmir. He smiled and said " People are put into unnecessary fight because of Kashmir.Saab people need bread. No body likes fight.

I said " you are very much right." Our journey was started again. We crossed Jhelum and were crossing Dina bypass. Our mini bus was running in rhythm leaving villages and blocks behind. During this journey we saw many army trucks loaded with Jawans, sometimes taking side from our mini bus and sometimes crossing from opposite side of the road. It was 7p.m in the evening and we were crossing through Manglapur road.

From moving bus we saw great Bungalows and excellent buildings. I understand that we had entered in Mirpur. Our Mini Bus stopped near press club at Mirpur. We were welcomed with garland by the honourable people of Mirpurs. After offering evening Namaj, we were called for breakfast. They had managed both Non-vegetarian and vegetarian food so we had a choice there. After breakfast we were introduced with honorable and respected people of Mirpur. There, we discussed about next day program.

We were accommodated in two star hotel named JABIR. There I saw a good crowd keep coming to meet us. It was an interesting fact that when people of Mirpur knew that

People from India's Jammu and Kashmir had visited their place, they did not stop themselves to meet us. We were talking to locals even at 2 a.m in night. Few locals gifted me books in Urdu and English language. They also discussed about under construction Mangla Dam and controversies related to it.

Now I must tell you something about Mirpur. India got independence on the basis of two nation theory and divided into two parts creating one more nation Pakistan.

During this period communal hatred remained on top of every body's mind. Taking benefits of these circumstances, Pakistan captured Mirpur illegally. Pakistan has been looking after all the administrative works of this region under the agreement of United Nation Organization signed in 1949 . Pakistan holds supreme power here. Natural beauty, hills and forests are the assets of Mirpur and entire kotli region. Mirpur and kotli are two small district of Pakistan Occupied Kashmir. This region of Pakistan Occupied Kashmir is very important from war point of view and very sensitive from the point of view of Indo-Pakistani relationship. This part of Pakistan Occupied Kashmir has its border attached to Naushera sector of Jammu region of India. In this part of Pakistan Occupied Kashmir, India and Pakistan is divided only with Line of Control. From the Line of Control to 16 kilometers area of Pakistan Occupied Kashmir has been declared high security zone by Government of Pakistan. This part of Pakistan Occupied Kashmir is hundred percent protected area and even foreign journalists are not allowed to enter into this part of Pakistan Occupied Kashmir. If any foreign journalist wants to come this part of Pakistan Occupied Kashmir as tourists then he/she has to take no objection certificate from the Ministry of Kashmir Affairs situated in capital Islamabad. He/She is supposed to mention the

Author along with Pakistani Intellectuals in a seminar at Mirpur

places to visit. In one line, administration of Pakistan don't allow any foreigner to visit this part of Pakistan Occupied Kashmir. The region is obvious. There are dozens of Militant training camps run in this region. Here young People are being trained in handling guns, making bombs and other arts of terrorism. These Camps are being run by the ISI, Pakistani Army and other powerful terrorist organizations. All the terrorist camps run within the sphere of 15 kilometers of high security zone. The ISI and Pakistani Army first train young boys, then equipped them with Guns, Bombs and proper planning and then order them to cross Line of Control. They take care up to the moment Militants step in India crossing Line of Control. Actually this part of Pakistan Occupied Kashmir is encircled with hills and forests and thus make this area difficult to watch all the time on the long kilometers of Line of Control . Pakistan Army and the ISI have made many launching pads for sending Militants beyond Line of Control . Indian army always remain in pressure to check the movement of Militants on the Line of Control .

Before partition, this Mirpur was Hindu dominated area. Partition created one after another hell in this area. Kabaili attacked on Mirpur and killed maximum numbers of Hindu settled there. Hindu women had to face humiliation. At last all the Hindu families of Mirpur had to migrate from there. Most of the family reached Jammu and few in the other parts of India and settled there. Some of Hindu family had strong connections in foreign countries and they migrated overseas. With the passing time,these pictures of extreme pain and humiliation are almost erased from mind but when you reach here, your heart cries and your eyes shed tears. If you are an Indian and visits this part of Pakistan Occupied Kashmir, you may be mesmerized to see the natural beauty but if you know the history of this place, can not enjoy this ultimate beauty. You will try to discover the past of this place, will go in deep thought and may feel the pain and agonies of being killed with the family and being forced to migrate with the family. You can feel there kabaili attacking on you, sucking your blood and tearing the respect of the women of your family. I was seeing the beauty of this place thinking about its cruel past that uprooted entire Hindu community from its Motherland.

Mirpur is also famous for its Mangla Dam constructed on Jhelum river. We were informed that many villages were sink into water because of this Dam. This Dam is still a subject of big protest in Pakistan. We also came to know that a great historical temple of Goddess Mangla Devi was unsettled for forever during the construction of Mangla Dam .

We were not surprised to see big Bungalows and Kothis at Mirpur but we were surprised to see them locked. We found presence of hounding silence in most of the buildings. Later came to know that owner of those buildings were settled in foreign countries and leaved their bungalows in the hands of security guards. Some of security guards were living inside bungalows with their family utilizing servant quarters. Big Bungalows and Kothis were attracting the attention of onlookers. You see the beauty with open eyes and feel the hallucination of natural beauty with close eyes. Sudden I recalled my memory. Myself, being J and K Bureau Chief of Hindi News paper Rastriya Sahara had unfolded many sensational news related to this part of Pakistan Occupied Kashmir. This was the place where Army of Pakistan, the ISI and Heads of various leading terrorist organizations had jointly called a meeting in the year of 2000. After this meeting they had form Border Action Team (BAT). This BAT was formed to spread terror in India with various blasts and selected killings. According to a report of intelligence, Border Action Team was responsible to make action plans to commit an act of terrorism. BAT was also given responsibility to help trained terrorist in crossing Line Of Control and to have vigil on them while working in India. BAT worked with the coordination of Pakistani Army and the ISI. It has been observed that on the Line Of Control, Pakistani Army starts firing on Indian Army, Indian Army starts counter firing. In this way Pakistani army engages Indian army and BAT pushes trained terrorists beyond Line Of Control. This way terrorists enter into the soil of India and play their game of spreading terror. It is an open fact and still today infiltration is continued and hundreds of trained militants successfully get access into the land of India by crossing Line Of Control.

I had reported all these facts and it was published in Rastriya Sahara. Now I was seeing the most dangerous place with naked eyes where Militants were produced to spread terror in India. It is an open fact that Mirpur and Kotli region are the gateway of fundamentalist leaders, militants, terrorist organizations and all are being nourished by the ISI and Pakistani army. Money and all kinds of weapons, training materials and trainers are being provided by the ISI and Pakistani army.

■■■

Chapter 13

POK Wants Freedom from Pakistan

People of Mirpur are blessed with prosperity and intelligence. They speak Pahari, Dogri and Gojari dialects but Urdu is their official language. Mirpur is only place in entire POK where you can see plane area along with many tiny hills.At the distance of 16 kilometer of Mirpur and near Mangla Dam, a new town named Mangla has been developed.

Actually we media people were taken to Mirpur with a purpose. Our host Pakistan wanted to feed us with all the facts that go in their favour regarding POK and its people, their views about J & K and obviously about India. Though most of the

Pakistani Separatist leader Amanullah khan

people who came to meet us were sponsored by ISI and Army of Pakistan, yet we could able to meet with some of locals and found an anger inside them for Government of Pakistan. I preferred to interact with local people only. There I came on conclusion that youth of Mirpur were influenced with separist leader Amanullah Khan and Yasin Malik. Probably due to this reason youth of Pakistan occupied Kashmir carry some degree of anger against Government of Pakistan.

You can easily understand the interference of Pakistan Army and ISI on the lives of common citizens of Mirpur. Entire Mirpur is flooded with Pakistan Army, Rangers and ISI officials. Movement of trucks loaded with Army are common sites. ISI keeps bird's eye view on every possible movement of common people of this area. We were also sure that ISI must had a watch on us.

We journalists were accommodated in JABIR hotel. After the day's program when we returned back to hotel, saw a mob shouting slogans against Pakistan. Dictatorship flourish with dishonesty and wrong notions of dictators. Pakistan has remained solely responsible for pushing militants equipped with arms and training to spread terror in Indian state of Jammu & Kashmir. This policy of Pakistan was bouncing back in Pakistan occupied Kashmir. Youth and half aged people carrying mashal (flambeau) in hand were shouting slogans "we want freedom". They shout slogans continuous for 15 minutes and then vanished. Later we came to know that all protestors were residents of Mirpur. Actually protesters got an opportunity to loud their voice in front of journalists of both the Nations. They showed their anger against Government of Pakistan and also against Pak Army and ISI. They unfold a fact that administration had just provided electricity in the surrounding area of hotel to show a better Mirpur to Indian journalists, otherwise this area is destined to remain in darkness. Whatever I was informed that people who were shouting slogans, just wanted to show us the real picture of POK & Mirpur. This protest was a great blow on ISI? How ISI allowed them to carry a procession in front of Indian journalist remained a question for Government of Pakistan. Protestors were dispersed within 15 minutes of

INDIA KILLS US BY BULLET AND PAKISTAN DROWNS US

The Original construction of the Mangla in 60's was carried out against the expressed will of the people of Jammu Kashmir, it was enforced upon them under the threat of barrel of gun, and promises made by the government of Pakistan were never honoured.

The whole Mangla Dam project constitutes violations of basic human rights and sheer exploition of the people of Jammu Kashmir, moreover it is violation of International Law.

The proposed extension will leave 150,000 inocent people displaced, tens of thousands graves of our loved would further submerged under water, destruction of our heritage and major affect on wild life.

The proposed extension of Mangla Dam is huge conspiracy by the government of to uproot the entire people of Mirpur in order to complete their hidden agenda of division of Jammu Kashmir.

We pledge to our people that we would not let an inch of an extension carried out forcefully by the government of Pakistan through their white elephant WAPDA even if it means to secrifice our lives in order that we can protect the life and property of our people, safe guard the graves of our loved one, protect our remaining heritage and save the wild life.

May Allah help and guide us in JUST CAUSE

ANTI MANGLA DAM EXTENSION ACTION COMMITTEE

UK Office:
250, YARDLEY WOOD ROAD, MOSELEY, BIRMINGHAM B13 9JN. UK.
Tel: 0121-442 4544 Fax: 0121-449 5294 e-mail: antimangladam@aol.com
Mirpur Office:
P.O. Chaksawari, Dist. Mirpur, Jammu Kashmir.
Tel: Chaksawari Exchange: 375 / 03005 112273 Fax: 0303 6980493

The book published on Mangla Dam

Arrival of Indian journalists in Mirpur had become a subject of discussion amongst locals of Mirpur. They were excited to meet us. It was the first opportunity since 57 years when a team of Indian journalist had visited this place. People of Mirpur wanted to share their emotions with us. Some of them gave us books printed in Urdu language. One of Dr. Abdul Aziz told me that his rest of the family live in Rajouri Village, beyond line of control in India. Dr. Abdul Aziz still had a hope to meet his family members living in India and his last wish was to touch the soil where he was born. Dr. Abdul Aziz also revealed a fact that was shocking for me and could be heartbreaking for you. About 20 lakh family of Mirpur and kotla region are separated from their kith & kin. They breath in anger and sleep with tears in eyes. I was surprised to see the reaction of people at ground Zero. All want freedom, all want free movement to meet their families living across line of control....but no one listen them. A senior citizen informed us that they believes in non-violence and put their voice in that manner only. I took the name of Mahatma Gandhi. He said " Yes we follow Mahatma here".

■■■

Chapter 14

Searching for Freedom

We had a short stay at Mirpur. We had been told that next day in afternoon we had to proceed towards capital city Islamabad. At Mirpur we had been given room in hotel JABIR. There we met many people who were in favor of freedom movement in Indian state of Jammu & kashmir. But when I asked them " Why Pakistan never think about giving freedom to POK".

They had no answer. Actually this was the time when the whole world had seen free & fair election in the Indian state of Jammu & Kashmir and the state Government was formed with the clear mandate given by people. Why this kind of election never happened in Pakistan occupied Kashmir? They had no answer. I put another question ? If leaders of Pakistan ever wanted to have peace & friendly relation across line of control, then why they pump terrorist through line of control in Indian territory? Why this high security zone of POK are converted into Military Cantonment and training camps of militants? Nobody had answer of my questions.

They kept mum or smiled in defeat. In all our discussions with intellectuals, politicals leaders & local representatives at Mirpur , a hard truth came with a bang that POK wanted to get rid of Pakistan. We all know that Pakistan have been doing propaganda that undivided

Kashmir along with POK want to merge in Pakistan. But we found POK shouting slogans freedom from Pakistan. Dictator General Parwej Musharraff had given a formula to divide undivided Jammu-Kashmir into seven parts and it was thoroughly rejected by the people of POK. No body gave second thought on this formula while discussing with us.

People in POK now talk about complete freedom of both the undivided Kashmir and Pakistan occupied kashmir. They say our's part is called Azad Jammu-Kashmir but where is the freedom ? That part is under rule of India and this part is under rule of Pakistan. In India's Jammu - Kashmir democracy prevails, so they are in better condition and POK is under rule of Pakistani Army and ISI so they are in worst condition. Here in POK only those citizen can cast vote who accepts complete merger of Azad Jammu-Kashmir in Pakistan.

Everybody supposed to fill a form of such acceptance before casting his/her vote. People of POK ask for freedom and Pakistan forces for merger.

Before 1947 entire Jammu-Kashmir was undivided and was under the rule of Maharaja Hari Singh. People of this region demands complete

Secretary of Jammu and Kashmir League & former Chief Justice of Azad Jammu and Kashmir Janab Abdul Mazeed Malik.

An Encounter with Pakistan's Reality

freedom of that undivided Jammu-Kashmir. People of this region also want to get back those lands of Jammu-Kashmir which was given to china. They say, Where is Kashmir ? We have been captured from all corners. Some parts are under the rule of India, some parts Pakistan has captured and some parts have been given to china by Pakistan.

I need your attention of these facts ? Entire land area of Jammu-Kashmir is 2,222,236 sq. Kilometers. Out of this land Pakistan has illegally captured a land of 78,000 sq. kilometers. Earlier this land was under Indian territory. Pakistan rules this land under Karanchi agreement signed in 1949. Pakistan occupied Kashmir (POK) is divided into two parts. First part has the land area of 5,703 sq. kilometer and is called Azad Jammu-Kashmir. Second part has the land area of 72,49659 sq. kilometer and is called Northern area. This area was illegally captured by Pakistan during partition of India in 1947.

This Northern Area has been divided into five districts by Pakistan to have better administration. These districts are Gilgit, Sakdur, Damir, Chhijer and Ghanje. This Northern Area is bordered with Afghanistan in one side, North west frontier Pakistan in second side and China on the third Side. This way Northern area is cornered from all three sides with Afghanistan, Pakistan & China . People of Azad Jammu-Kashmir consider this northern area as their land.

This is a matter of great concern that apart from loud protest of India, Pakistan had given a land of 5180sq. kilometer to China in 1963 under an agreement on border issue between them. An Indian land was captured Pakistan and illegally delivered to another Nation.

India could not stop this transaction & still today raises this issue on every possible platform.

I got an opportunity to meet Chief Justice of Azad Jammu-Kashmir & President of Jammu-Kashmir Liberation League Janab Abdul Aziz Malik. He was appreciating both the nations India & Pakistan for the steps being taken by them to solve Kashmir problem. He was very much clear in his mind and wanted freedom from both India & Pakistan.

■■■

Chapter 15

Destiny of the People of Mirpur

Memory of Mirpur can not be completed without discussing Mangla Dam Project. There is a popular belief that when people fight for freedom, criticize every move of ruler. People of Azad Jammu-Kashmir are fed up with Government of Pakistan and openly demand freedom form Pakistan Government. They remain in search of

Mangla Dam of Mirpur

opportunity to raise their voice on international forum. Their urge to achieve freedom can be seen in various protests against Government of Pakistan. River Jhelum crosses from Mirpur. Government of Pakistan made a dam on this river and confined floating water into grand big pond. This dam is named after Goddess Mangla and is called Mangla Dam. People say that Temple of Goddess Mangla was ruined during making of Mangla Dam. Controversy is the another face of Mangla Dam. Now Government of Pakistan have given permission for its extension and it is also being protested heavily. Situation of Mirpur has been worsening every day. People's voice against Mangla Dam have become movement of freedom of Azad Jammu-Kashmir. People of Azad Jammu-Kashmir have raised their voice against Mangla Dam even in united Nations and it other international forums. Mangla Bandh Vistar Virodhi Sangharsh Samiti (A Society Against extension of Mangla Dam) have unfolded those facts that Pakistan always kept secret. This society also have its wing in Birmingham, England and they use to put their voice of freedom on international forums in very systematic way. They blame on Pakistan for unnecessary interference in entire Azad Jammu-Kashmir. The propaganda of Pakistan that Azad Jammu-Kashmir want to merge in Pakistan have been proved many times total lie by people of Azad Jammu-Kashmir.

The members of the society, who are fighting against the extension planning of Mangla Dam, had come to meet with Indian journalist. They shed their emotions and detailed about their movement of freedom. Though ISI tried to stop them from having any interaction with us but they took risk and met us. The society members given us a book dedicated to freedom of POK written in Urdu and English. Here I want to give a glimpse of front page of this book. It reads as " India kills us with bullet, Pakistan kills us by drowning into water". Project Mangla Dam had been started in 1960 kicking out big protest of people of Mirpur. Government of Pakistan had promised to provide better life to the people of Mirpur just to get support in favour of making Mangla Dam but never fulfill a single promise. Pakistan had openly violated fundamental human rights. Govt. of Pakistan made Mangla Dam keeping entire people of Mirpur on point of gun.

Extension of Mangla Dam will make homeless to 1,50,000 innocent people and approx ten thousand graves will be drown into water. It all are against humanity. Extension of Mangla Dam will also ruin our culture, our heritage and our wild life. This extension planning of Manglapur is conspiracy against people of Mirpur to unsettle them permanently from Mirpur. Extension of Mangla Dam is a part of those secret plans under which Govt. of Pakistan is preparing divide Azad Jammu & Kashmir. We take Oath that we will not allow Government of Pakistan to take even an inch of our land. Though this government is going to handover this work in the hands of white elephant, Water and Development Authority. We are ready to save property and lives of common people even at the cost of our lives. We have to keep our graveyards safe; we have to preserve our heritage and wild life.

We pray to Allah to give us power to fight against inhuman and draconian government of Pakistan. Now I want to attract your attention on next page of this book. It reads as " Here in Mangla Dam electricity is generated with the blood, meet, fat and bones of the people of Azad Jammu Kashmir.

Dam was constructed on the Graveyards. Now any plan of its extension could be completed only on the dead body of the people of Azad Jammu Kashmir.

This book has been complied with historical facts also. According to this book " in 1904 King of of Dogra and Govt. of state Punjab had signed an agreement on river Jhelum to construct a Dam on it. It was the period when Rajput King Hari Singh were the sole ruler of entire undivided Kashmir.

This book also details about the agreement signed between Govt. of Azad Jammu-Kashmir and Water and Power Development Authority on 27 June, 2003.

Shamshad Hussain a lawyer of Rawalkot, Pakistan has written an article titled " Mangla Dam and united Nations organization. This book details all the appeals filed by people of POK in United Nations against the construction of Mangla Dam. Picture of atrocities of army of Pakistan along with the inhuman approach of govt. of Pakistan also has been projected in this book.

On 30July 2001, the then President General Perwej Musharraf had given his consent on this controversial Mangla Dam extension project. Pakistan government itself had given the approx. number of displaced people because of the extension planning of Mangla Dam.

On 30 september, 2001, President General Parwej Musharraf had visited Mirpur to inaugurate the extension planning of Mangla Dam. People gathered in thousands in protest even General was in air on chartered Army Helicopter. People shouted slogans against General and faced tear gas and lathi charge by police and paramilitary forces. Later protesters also became violent and started pelting stones converting place of inauguration into land of war. Government had promised during the proposal of this Mangla Dam in 1960 that all the displaced people will be rehabilitated in Pakistan. Very few were rehabilitated in Pakistan but without basic amenities. Actually govt. of Pakistan wanted to shift most of the families of Mirpur from its land to exploit the natural resources uninterrupted. When people of POK demand their rights, they are ignored with the logic that it does come under the law of their nation. People of this region are destined to face the pain and agonies erupted because of Mangla Dam. At one hand Pakistan continuously has been exploiting the people of Pakistan Occupied Kashmir and on the other hand it has been sponsoring militant training camps in the highly security zone of POK. Trained militants with Pakistan sponsored bullets & bombs kill innocent people of India. Unending terrorism in India is being nourished at Azad Jammu & Kashmir.

■ ■ ■

Chapter 16
Mirpur: An Example of Brotherhood

Even before partition of 1947, Mirpur with the river Jhelum in its lap was a prosperous town. I found some untold stories buried behind today's prosperous Mirpur. Just after partition of India, this part of Pakistan occupied Kashmir, the then was the part of undivided Kashmir, had faced extreme of torture and violence.

Panoramic View of Mirpur

Before the attack of armed kabaili infiltrators, this Mirpur region was a great example of communal harmony and mutual friendship. If we dig the history of Mirpur, some great facts will come out of it. During 600-650B.C. a Muslim saint Meer Shah Gazi and a Hindu Sanit Gosai Bodhpuri had blessed this region. This region was named taking first name of Muslim saint and the last name of Hindu saint and was called Mirpur. But this great historical background was tormented drastically. Armed Kabailis attackers brutally killed almost 70 percent population of Hindu and Sikh amongst total population of twenty five thousands. Women were dishonored. Whoever survived were heavily wounded. Senior citizens of Mirpur still narrate the horrible stories of kabaili attackers. This incident is printed as Mirpurkand (killings in Mirpur) in history.

Here I must tell you that this Mirpur plays greater role in defaming India along with Pakistan . Actually a good number of Mirpurians live in foreign countries and they send money to keep movement alive against India. Now they also started raising their voices against government of Pakistan. It was the last day of our stay at mirpur. We had yet to meet a lot of people. I could not had sound sleep in last night. Whole night I remained engulfed with emotional thoughts told by the people of Mirpur. In earlier chapter I discussed about a senior citizen of POK Nasirullah, who cried in front of me and had shown his last wish to meet his family member living in India's Kashmir at Rajouri village. I met many such Nasirullah who crossed line of control in deception and could not returned back to their roots. Mirpur is flooded with such kind of people. People of Kotli region carry a certain level of anger against government of Pakistan. Electricity is generated in Mirpur and utilized in Pakistan. A lot of Pakistan sponsored militants camps are being run in kotli region to spread terror in India. This Mirpur region is closer to line of control and geographically encircled with many tiny hills and thus Pakistan has selected this region to operate militants training camps to spread terror in India.

Here I recall words of Saint BulleShah –

Apna Dass Thikana, Kidharon Aaya Kidhar Jana,

Jis Thane ka maan Karen tu, ohave naal na jana.

Julm Karen to lok satave,

Kasub fariyaon loot khana.

Kar laichawar chaar dihare,

Orak to uttth jane.

A very rare picture of Bulle Shah

(O' creature ! From where you belong ? From where you have come and where you have to go?Nothing will go with you in heaven. You commit crime & torture people. You can have a false proud for few days but at last you have to leave this planet.)

These lines perfectly suit to those people who are engaged in spreading terror and killing of innocent people.

Here we found a clear picture. Government of Pakistan, Army of Pakistan and ISI all make false statements regarding India, create hardship for the people of Pakistan occupied Kashmir and exploit natural resources of this region and utilizes this part of Azad jammu-Kashmir to spread terror in India. No

An Encounter with Pakistan's Reality

body denies this hard fact. Many times it had resulted into big Indo-Pak tension and became a reason behind Indo-Pak war. When terrorists had attacked on parliament of India on 13 december 2001, terrorist camps of this area was blamed directly. Once India's leadership had decided to destroy all these militants camps of POK but could not implement its planning because of fear of nuclear war and international pressure.

Pakistan also accepts the existence of various militants training camps in kotla region. General Parwej Mushrraf had accepted these facts in one of his speech given on 12 January 2001. He said " If India gives us guarantee for not creating a war like situation, we can close all the militant training camps running in the Pakistan occupied Kashmir, to have better relationship in between both the countries". Actually we journalist were taken to Pakistan occupied Kashmir by the government of Pakistan to feed us only those facts that suit them.

This visit was co-sponsored by army of Pakistan and ISI. They wanted to see us interacting only with sponsored people rather than common people of this place.

Apart from meeting all those sponsored people and organizations, we also found common people trying hard to meet us to unfold their genuine thought and state of mind. Almost in every meeting and every interaction, subjects like extension of Mangla Dam, undivided Jammu & Kashmir and freedom movement remained in focus.

A local resident Asfaque Hussain informed us regarding upbringing of terrorist (Mujahids) in the name of freedom movement (Jehad). Before I asked next question to him, few people came and take him out from the venue. It was clear that those people, who took away Asfaque Hussain, were ISI people. Later ISI people tried to know that what Asfaque was informing me. I simply said he was taking something about extension of Mangla Dam.

Where ever I went and to whoever I met at Mirpur, all indicated in mask voice that kotla region was being utilized in running various militant training camps. We were taken in a meeting at district bar council of Mirpur. There we saw banners and posters reflecting demands of complete freedom. One of speaker Prof. Nazeer blamed both the Nations India & Pakistan for giving importance of Hurriyat conference. According to him Hurriyat conference can not solve problem of Kashmir as they are confined to a limited area. It will be better to invite all the communities of Jammu-Kashmir either they are Hindu, Sikh or Buddh for dialogue. One of human right activist Zameer Mirza showed his great concern on the migration of Kashmir pundits and thoroughly criticized it. He also revealed that most of the political leaders, social organizations and intellectuals don't recognize " All party Hurriyat conference" as the real representative of Jammu-Kashmir. Hurriyat conference works only in India's Kashmir and thus it become essential to invite people of all class and communities for dialogue to achieve permanent solution of Kashmir problems.

■■■

Chapter 17
Mirpur Fort

While we were in Lahore, General Parwej Musharraf had said that Hurriyat conference must be given importance in peace dialogues. We tried to take opinion on this issue from locals of Mirpur. Mirpur press club had organized a meeting with some of fundamentalist leaders. Many fundamentalist leaders put their voice on Kashmir. Banner were displaced in Urdu language so I had to take help from my fellow Urdu knowing Journalist. An Organization of Azad Jammu-Kashmir "Jamate-Ulema" were welcoming all the journalists who were concern to solve Kashmir

Water of Mangla Dam touching Mirpur Forte

problem. One another banner was reflecting the mind set of the people of POK that they were against the division of Jammu-Kashmir. These banners and posters were showing the changed mind set of people of this region. It was proved that propaganda of Pakistan on international forums that people of POK want to merge in Pakistan was nothing but a baseless statement.

I tried to come out with information regarding various militant training camps in Kotla region while interacting with the common people of Mirpur. At one hand I found that common people of this region wanted to have better relationship with India and also dream about restructuring of Jammu-Kashmir and on the other hand fundamentalism was being nourished. Govt. of Pakistan, Army and ISI had kept us in fool proof management where it was really hard to interact with common people and to know about militants training camps.

Though few people tried to give us information in disguised voice. According to them, training camps of militants groups like Lashkar-e-taiba, Hisbul mujahidin, Hisbul mujahidin pir panjal range etc were active since years in Mirpur & Kotla region.

This region is highly sensitive because of these militant training camps. You would not get much in Mirpur that was modern in outlook. Yes ultimate natural beauty alone is enough to fascinate every one. We were taken to a famous place which was at the distance of 8 kilometer from Mirpur, named Khari sharif. Here we saw Shrine of famous Sufi saint Baba Pir-e-Shah Gazi. There was a Islamic education center located near this shrine. Here we also met some of Darwesh (follower of sufi saint baba Pir E Shah Gazi). They all were divine in appearance. We had given a description of fort by department of tourism. This fort was named Mirpur fort. Earlier it was named Rampur Fort. This fort was encircled with hills from three sides and constructed in the lap of river Jhelum. Here an ancient Shiv temple was in existence and it had appeared during a excavation. Two big ponds & shrine of Muslim Saint Tughlaki Baba were also in existence with Shiv emple. This Rampur fort or Mirpur fort was situated near the Mangla Lake and in the opposite direction of Mirpur. One could reach this fort by boat only. This place was under control of Pakistan army, though it was being highlighted as tourist place.

Here, again I want to discuss Mangla Dam. Entire Mangla Dam and its surround is nothing less than a tourist place. Whoever comes Mirpur,definitely visit Mangla Dam. Actually earlier entire area was

Satish Verma with Salim Pandit (journalist) at Mirpur

known as Mirpur kotla. In 1975 Mirpur Kotla was divided into Mirpur and Kotla. At present Kotli is a district of POK. Kotli is known as place of beautiful Mosques and hot spring called as Tatta Paani. It is belived that a bath in Tatta paani cures all the skin diseases.

Apart from Tatta paani Kotli attracts people because of its tourist places like ' Kohi Raata', Gulpur and few other places that are full of immense natural beauty.

Like Mirpur, Kotli also has a fort constructed at 1460. People say various stories about this fort. Few people say that Dogra Army headed by Col. Mahmood was confined by locals into this Thorochi fort. Most of the soldiers of Dogra army killed and very few, who had enough arms, could able to reach Jammu. In the memory of killed soldiers, martyrs memorials had been erected in Dabripur and at present it is the most important place of Azad Jammu-kashmir. When I came to know about this monuments, I wanted to visit Dabripur but it was not planned in our schedule. I felt helpless. Later I knew that some terrorist camps were active at Dabripur and our movement at that place was impossible.

■■■

An Encounter with Pakistan's Reality

Chapter 18

Azad Jammu and Kashmir: Divided into Pieces

It is an irony for divided Jammu and Kashmir that a common Indian understands that it is divided into two parts only. One part is under control of Pakistan and second part is a constitutional state of India. But actually Jammu and Kashmir is divided into three pieces. One piece belongs to Azad Jammu and Kashmir, second belongs to Gilgit to which Pakistan says Northern part. People of Azad Jammu and Kashmir takes Gilgit as their part because it was undivided before 1947. Pakistan had captured this land and now trying to project it as its integral part and the third piece of land Kashmir was delivered to China by Pakistan. Pakistan first captured this land illegally and then transferred it to China under a border agreement signed between them. Now people of Azad Jammu and Kashmir started raising their voice against this Pak-China deal and want to get back their land.

Still today Pakistan is not able to justify constitutionally that Northern part is an integral part of Pakistan. Pakistan shows its right on Northern part of undivided Jammu and Kashmir because of the agreement known as "The Karanchi 1949" Agreement. "The Karanchi 1949" was signed by the Government of Pakistan, President of Azad Jammu and

Kashmir and President of all Jammu & Kashmir Muslim conference. But this fact is not even half truth. The only truth is that since 1 july 1950, Govt. of Pakistan have been ruling on this Northern part of undivided Kashmir illegally and unconstitutionally.

One of books, that gifted to author at Mirpur

"Karanchi 1949" agreement lost its sanctity when Azad Jammu and Kashmir act 1970 came in existence. Later Azad Jammu and Kashmir constitution act 1974 took place and seized the sanctity of all earlier agreements. Government of Pakistan remained pioneer in making and signing above all the agreements.

Azad Jammu and Kashmir including Northern part of undivided Jammu and Kashmir are not the legal part of Pakistan. And because of this reason Pakistan neither announced that these part are their integral part nor say that they are doing patronage of this Northern part.

No any national or international law gives right to any nation to rule on a piece of land without any constitutional parameter. Constitutionally Pakistan is not ruling on the undivided Northern part but it controls on this part through its ministry of Kashmir and Northern region affairs. This way this entire region is being govern by Pakistan. Resident

An Encounter with Pakistan's Reality

commissioner is being appointed by Govt. Of Pakistan and only a citizen of Pakistan is appointed as Resident commissioner of Gilgit or Northern region. Pakistan has clear cut policy to capture Northern region of undivided Kashmir, which has land area of 72,495 sq. kilometre. Pakistan has also been trying to appease the citizen of Azad Jammu and Kashmir by declaring it Azad state. It has a land area of only 5,703 sq. kilometre. Pakistan has been successfully handling these situations and it seems that one day Pakistan will succeed in its efforts.

Government of Pakistan is in false confidence that if this matter will be raised in United Nations, they will win the situation with their political power. People of Azad Jammu and Kashmir have come to know the game plan of Pakistan and started raising their voice for complete freedom. They want complete freedom of United Jammu and Kashmir along with the land. delivered to China.

People of Jammu and Kashmir now fully understand that China has taken bigger benefit out of theirs conflict. Pakistan wanted to had an upper hand on India and thus in the greed of getting support of China's army power, handed over a piece of land acquired illegally. China maintains cool on this issue and say that the Pakistan delivered that piece of land under an agreement and this is a temporary transaction not permanent one. On 25th march 1963, foreign department of China has written a letter to the embassy of India clearing that Kashmir is a problem between India & Pakistan and China is not part of that. When India & Pakistan will come on final solution of Kashmir problem then China will try to solve the border problem through dialogue. This way China has captured the land. China knew that India and Pakistan will never reach on any permanent solution on Kashmir issue.

Whatever I must come on the conclusion of Mirpur, Kotli visit. Apart from all the planning of Government of Pakistan, ISI and Pakistan army to keep us away from common people of Mirpur, we got an opportunity to meet & interact with them and knew the reality of that place, person and circumstances.

We listened them and cleared our doubts and reached a certain conclusion. We had a very busy schedule at Mirpur. After Mirpur we had to visit Islamabad. Though we wanted to spend some more time at Mirpur, but it was impossible. We were grateful to the Government of Pakistan for providing us with an opportunity to meet various people of Mirpur and Kotli region.

Earlier I had seen the beauty of India's Jammu and Kashmir and now have been seeing beauty of Azad Jammu and Kashmir. Why Kashmir is called heaven on Earth I got answer.. Journey to Islamabad had begun. We were reaching capital of Pakistan Islamabad. I knew that Islamabad was one of the most beautiful and planned city of the world, as Mirpur is called Mirpur-Kotli, Islamabad is called Islamabad-Rawalpindi.

■ ■ ■

Chapter 19
Pakistan Assembly

Islamabad. A grand city of Pakistan. A well planned modern and beautiful capital of Pakistan. Islamabad came in limelight in 1958 when Ayub Khan was the president of Pakistan.

Karanchi is known as economic center of Pakistan and Islamabad is the political center. Rawalpindi is an another important city located just next to Islamabad in the map of

National Assembly of Pakistan

Pakistan. Rawalpindi had remained the main city of business activities of Sikh business men in 19th century. Britain captured Rawalpindi during second Sikh war. In 1849 British made this city an army headquarters of north region. Along with low and middle class people, rich and liberal people also live in great number in Rawalpindi. From hardcore fundamentalists to extremists, all have homes in Rawalpindi. Pakistan is a Muslim Nation and it is also a Muslim dominated Nation but still has different perception about Islam. Pakistan has two different faces – one face shows its liberal and secular nature and other face depicts Islamic fundamentalism & extremism. One face represents Islamabad and other face represents Rawalpindi. Both are twin city but opposite to each other. Islamabad is growing with the growing speed of population and the same thing happening with Rawalpindi and it is expected that growing population will convert both the cities in one

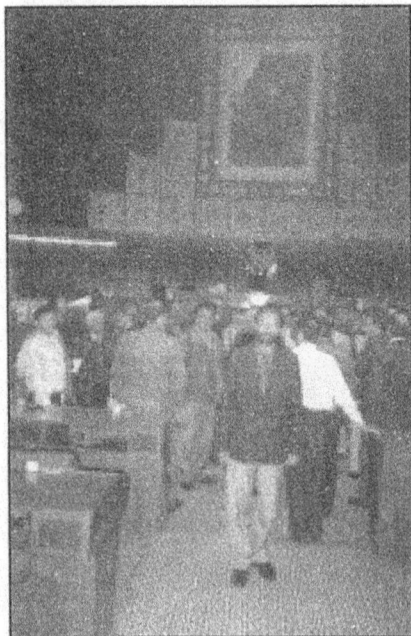

big city. But still today both the cities are quite opposite in inheritance, heritage and personality. Islamabad came in existence with the modern approach of twentieth century and Rawalpindi grew into a city from an old backward village.

Islamabad is a well planned city with wide roads & grand buildings with modern architecture and Rawalpindi is a city of narrow streets & crowded old grand buildings.

Author inside Pakistan national assembly

Rawalpindi is also birth place of the then president of Pakistan, General Parwej Musharraf.

I also came to know that Rawalpindi also have great archaeological importance. Relic of an ancient Baudh University Takshshila was found in an archaeological excavation. Historian says that this place has become invaluable for the followers of Baudh religion. This university was spread in almost 25 kilometer and was in existence during 6th century B.C. It is also said that in 326 B.C. the great Sikander had entered in India through this root. The great King Ashoka had constructed Takshshila University for the study of Buddhism. At present in Pakistan, this Takshshila University is called Texla. British administration had chosen city Rawalpindi to establish its biggest Army Cantonment. Even today Rawalpindi is the headquarter of Pakistan Army. In 1947, India got independence with two Nations theory and a new state Pakistan was born. Every Nation needs a capital and to choose a capital city became a biggest problem for the leaders of newly born state Pakistan. Lahore was close to Indo-Pak border, and Karachi was too far from other famous cities. Actually they wanted their capital city somewhere in the middle of the nation and at last all were agree to make capital city of Pakistan near Rawalpindi. In 1950 Rawalpindi was chosen as capital city of Pakistan; and after a lot of thoughts and planning's in 1960 new capital city went under renovation and a Greek company was given contract to make this city in phases. In 1961 this new city started getting new face and was named Islamabad.

The first Government building was completed on 26 October 1966 in this grand city. Now this city Islamabad was ready to carry responsibility to capital city.

Rawalpindi was being used as temporary capital city and with much fan fare was shifted to Islamabad. When we entered in Islamabad, saw few grand buildings, wide roads and some very attractive places. Architecture of Supreme Court was ultramodern; and beauty of Shah Faizal Mosque was ultimate. City Islamabad was decorated with many gardens.

Chairman of Kashmir committee of Pakistan, Shree Hameed Chatdha

We were accommodated in "Holiday inn Hotel", a five star hotel in Islamabad. We had very busy schedule in Islamabad. We were taken to National Assembly of Pakistan. There we met with Chairman of Karachi committee, Hamid Kasir Chattha inside Parliament building.

On this occasion we also met with Information & Broadcasting Minister Shekh Rashid Ahmed.

We had a formal talk with the chairman of Kashmir committee Janab Hamid. He was almost against the division of Kashmir into seven parts, once suggested by General Parwej Musharraf. Janab Hamid said that already we had signed an agreement in United Nation that

An Encounter with Pakistan's Reality

problems of Kashmir would be sorted out with peaceful dialogues. He forcefully said that "Armed struggle in India's Jammu-Kashmir must get end because dialogues between both the nation was heading towards positive direction. People of both the nations now started getting opportunity to interacts one-another and this process must be utilized to achieve solution of Kashmir problem. Janab Hamid also showed indication towards giving an importance of Kashmiri leaders in peace talks in-between India & Pakistan. Though he also said that representatives of other groups might be called to reveal their opinion during peace dialogue. Janab Hamid strongly said that entire South Asia is under fire because of issue of Kashmir. Replying a question, he said that a bill was passed in United Nations that problem of Kashmir would be solved only through peaceful dialogues.

Further janab Hamid said that Government of Pakistan is not answerable for any act and decision taken by Ministry of Kashmir Affairs. They have their own parliament that constitutes national assembly & upper house with 48 committee members. This committee is responsible for taking any decision on Kashmir issue. He showed his anger with the words that both Nations must curtail budget of defense and put their maximum money for the developmental works.

At the end janab Hamid again put his voice very strongly that Kashmiri leaders must be taken as third party in every peace talks and then a permanent solution could be achieved. He openly said that terrorism could not be stopped unless and until through peace talks some permanent solution was achieved. During our conversation, few members of Kashmir committee were also present there.

■■■

Chapter 20
Searching for Their Thought

It was already decided that journalist from India will got opportunity to interexchange their thoughts with the media of Pakistan during Islamabad visit. I was anxiously waiting for this moment. This program was organized in a big hall in Hotel's basement. I just inform you that ISI of Pakistan keeps maintaining pressure on some segments of Pakistani media to keep alive their agenda against India. They have been doing propaganda that Indian media under the influence of Government of India have been writing against Pakistan. Media of Pakistan approves this false propaganda of ISI and it reflected during inter-exchange of thought program. Program started on time and everything was just right, suddenly an Indian journalist asked "Why not government of Pakistan ever invites media of Pakistan and take them on the line of control for actual reporting as Government of India and Indian army routinely take Indian media on line of control for reporting. Media people of Pakistan reacted sharply. They could not hide their anger and replied in harsh words. " Who are you to teach us. We know how to do coverage...and we know everything". It was not the end of their reaction. They even blamed on Indian media that they dance on the tune of their Ministry Of Foreign Affairs and blindly follow the briefing given by the Foreign Ministry.

पाक के कब्जे वाले कश्मीर में मुहाजिरों की दुर्दशा

Situation were worsening very fast. I stood from my seat and requested them to allow me to speak. I got permission and then requested to all of them to maintain cool. I also clarified that Indian journalists do respect their profession and never write anything or telecast anything under the influence of any power. I also gave an example.

It was a story of Amir Ali. Amir Ali was a 23 year young boy and was a student of third year in an engineering college in Pakistan. This ambitious young man made a biggest mistake of his life. He entered in Indian territory by crossing line of control. It was a mistake for Amir Ali and a crime in the eye of national & international laws. Amir Ali was caught by Indian border security force. Indian BSF took him as spy of Pakistan and interrogated him like an enemy and then handed over to the law of the Nation. Amir Ali was sentenced for 1 year imprisonment and send to jail.

Amir Ali was a resident of village Kadirbad situated in Syalkot region. Village kadirabad is located very near to the line of control. On 28 december 2001, Amir Ali

एक भूल ने कर दी इंजीनियर बनने की ख्वाहिश चकनाचूर

एक भूल ने कर दी इंजीनियर...

☐ भूल से भारतीय क्षेत्र में चला
आने का पाक का आरोप
☐ एक साल की सजा काटने के
बावजूद पड़ा है जेल में

unknowingly crossed line of control and entered into Indian territory at Ramgarh sector. It happened when he was having a long walk. This negligence ruined his life totally. Parents and family members of Amir Ali, searched him everywhere in Pakistan and then sensed a worse incidence that he could have crossed the line of control. Common citizen of either nation can not reach to the administrative people of either nation. So it became very difficult for parents of Amir Ali to approach Indian BSF or Indian Government to know where about of Amir Ali. Then they approached a human right activist Aasma Jehangir of Pakistan. Aasma Jehangir after going in the deep of this case, made a call

An Encounter with Pakistan's Reality

to a senior journalist of Jammu (India) Balraj Puri. Balraj Puri then was a coordinator of a human right organization called People's Union For Civil Liberties. Balraj puri also went in the deep of entire story of Amir Ali and then then immediately called me to reach at this residence Karan Nagar, in Jammu. He narrated me entire story of Amir Ali and put me on duty to search him at any cost. Yes, he also ordered his son Lav to help me in this mission.

Lav Puri was then bureau chief of "The Hindu" at Jammu Branch. It was a case of deserted family who had lost their young boy so we started searching Amir Ali to keep human emotions alive and to serve humanity whatever the little we could do. It was hard to search Amir Ali without any proper source in Jammu. Firing in darkness never works. I and Lav Puri made a proper planning to search Amir Ali. At first we reached Ramgarh sector which was very much closer to the line of control. After reaching Ramgarh sector, we first entered in Ramgarh police station and met with station-in-charge Jagdeep Barwal. We narrated him entire story. They supported our cause and went on searching files. Suddenly he informed us that a Pakistani young boy was arrested by Border security forces while he was crossing line of control and from August 02, 2002 he was under his custody. In excitement I took name of Amir Ali and station-in-charge Jagdeep Barwal confirmed us that the Pakistani boy who were under his custody was Amir Ali. It was a moment of joy for me and Lav. We were overjoyed.

We met with Amir Ali. Amir Ali looked lost his memory. He just had blind look at empty space. Mr. Jagdeep Barwal already had detailed about the mental condition of Amir Ali. We thought that Amir might take us as people of Indian intelligence, so we opened our heart and said him directly that his mother had send us. After completion of one year imprisonment Amir Ali was send under the custody of Ramgarh police station and from August 02, 2002, he was living there. Amir Ali was not co-operating with us. We tried hard to make him convinced that we were there to bail him out. We were feeling helpless.

When mobile phone service was started in Jammu, only selected people were getting connection. I was one amongst the few lucky person who were given connection of mobile phone in the first lot. My mobile rang up there. I saw the number. It was a call from Pakistan. It was just a co-incidence that we were in front of Amir Ali and got a call from Pakistan. I picked up the call and heard almost crying voice of Amir Mother " Satish saab…sathish saab mera beta mila (did you get my son)". I could not answer that Amir was in front of us because telephone was disconnected. It happened many times and puzzled us. At last we could able get proper connection and gave phone to Amir to say hello to his Mother. Amir talked to his Mother and looked relieved. Amir Ali written something for us. According to this information, he was bornon 4th April and wanted to complete his education of engineering if got passage to return back.

We were happy to find Amir Ali. Amir had completed his punishment. Now we had to work hard to send him back to his home at Pakistan. Only higher authority of state and central government could take the decision regarding sending Amir back to Pakistan. My phone was disconnected just after getting call from Pakistan. I got my connection back only after convincing higher authority that I was just helping an innocent person who were genuinely trapped in a wrong situation.

I wrote an article making Amir Ali as victim and published in our News Paper " Rastriya Sahara" and Lav also did reporting on Amir's case and published in " The

Hindu". Later this News was followed by most of the news papers including "Kashmir Times".

In my article I also discussed about two Pakistani adolescent boys Munir Ahmed and Shakeel Ahmed. Both had illegally entered in Indian terrory. Munir Ahmed could able to return back because the then Prime minister were trying hard to make better relationship with Pakistan. Along with some other Pakistani prisoner Munir Ahmed was also got opportunity to go back his home..Shakeel did not want to go back so he was allowed to live in India. Shakeel was feeling real freedom in India.

At last we were able to send Amir back to Pakistan and it was the most joyous moment for all of us.

I found all were relieved and felt relaxed after listening the story of Amir Ali and I was also satisfied that I had proved the credibility of Indian journalist. I could able to show them cuttings of News Papers proving truth of Amir's story. Actually I was carrying News Cuttings of some great reporting that could relate the emotions of both the countries. Later I distributed the photocopies of News Paper cuttings which had story of Amir Ali to all journalist of Pakistan.

Here I clearly understood that the Government of Pakistan, Pakistani Army and ISI have been misleading the common citizens of Pakistan by making false and fabricated stories against India.

■■■

Chapter 21
Wonderful Shah Faizal Mosque

How capital city Islamabad looks in night? It was in our thought and get fulfilled when Benazir's Pakistan people's party invited us for dinner. We were taken on a high hilly place after crossing spiral ways.

It was a famous Kashmiri restaurant with a feel of a roadside restaurant like dhaba. This place was known as

World famous Shah Faizal Mosque at Islamabad

Daman-e-Koh and was a famous picnic spot. Watching night view of Islamabad from top was an ultimate experience. Beauty of Islamabad lighted with street lights was hard to express in words. Though from Daman-e-Koh we could able to view entire Islamabad but world famous mosque of Islamabad Shah Faizal Mosque was clearly visible from there. Somebody told me that former President of Pakistan, General Zia-ul-Haque's body was cremated inside this Mosque and a Shrine was made on it inside the Shah Faizal Mosque. There was a building of international university of Islamic studies next to Shah Faizal Mosque. In restaurant we were served one after another tasty dishes. We thoroughly enjoyed the food and were thankful to Pakistan people's party for this grand treat.

Though we had a busy schedule yet Pak officers had made a plan to take us for seeing very important sights of Islamabad. We were taken to National Museum of Islamabad. This National Museum is dedicated to greatness of those people who hade been preserving art, tradition and heritage of Pakistan. This National Museum is spread in 60 thousand square feet and divided into many parts.

Most of the Museum of Pakistan are of archaeological importance but the National Museum of Islamabad is different from various angles. Materials from history, historical traditions, achievements of every class of people especially contributions of Kabailies and other achievements of various social groups are preserved here. Here in one hall we saw the most ancient artistic structure of 8000 B.C. that was related with the Harappa & Mohanjodaro civilization existed during 2500B.C.

These ancient structures were revealing the existence most ancient civilization. We entered in next hall and saw various musical instruments kept in tremendous conditions. Various ancient musical instruments were reflecting periods from veda to mohanjodaro civilization to modern Pakistani music.

Here we also saw well preserved materials reflecting Sufi traditions, paintings related to places of worship and other artistic samples connecting various cultural traditions of Pakistan. All were of historical importance.

In an another hall, materials related to traditional importance of kabaili and other various tribal groups were preserved. Hand made artistic & traditional cloths were preserved in a separate hall. Here we also saw collections of ancient jewelleries and handmade wood arts. We had little time to see this Museum but it was difficult to move your eyes and get out from the venue.

It was such an interesting and fascinating Museum that we were engulfed into it. At last we entered in a hall where memorable love stories were preserved in form of various paintings. Paintings of Heer-Ranjha & Dhola-Maaru had taken us is the sky of heavenly love & romance. There we also saw paintings reflecting love stories written by Hanishah-Murid. It all was a unforgettable experience.

The other most adorable and fascinating structure we saw in Islamabad was Shah Faizal Mosque. It was a great example of Modern architecture and was designed by famous architectural legend from Turkey named Vedant Dalok.

Shah Faizal Mosque was constructed in the area of 90 thousands square meter and was dedicated to Md. Faizal, late Sultan of Saudi Arab. The Tombs and Minars of this Mosque give a look of mystery. People say that Sultan of Saudi Arab Md. Faizal had given 5 crore dollar for the construction of this Mosque and thus was named Faizal Shah Mosque. Construction of this Mosque was started in

1976 and was completed in 1986. The whole world was surprised to see this Mosque which was designed extraordinarily.

America got confused to see the satellite picture of this Mosque and understood it as one of satellite launching center. American intelligence even wanted to see this Faizal mosque to clear their doubts.

■■■

Chapter 22
Changing Perceptions

We had to go long way in Islamabad but a lot of assumption and presumptions were already changed during this visit of Lahore. It was my second visit in Pakistan. Whatever I saw during the democratic rule of Miyan Nawaj Sharif found totally different in the army rule of General Parwej Musharraf. I found fundamentalism and extremism in Pakistan were rising high and it remained the most shocking perception of mine during this second visit. Nationalism was being defined with religious fundamentalism and because of this reason liberal leaders were subdued in Pakistan. Liberalism had no importance in front of religious fundamentalism. Cities of Pakistan like Islamabad & Rawalpindi were encircled with extremists and genuinely were heading towards blast. Before this visit of Pakistan, I had a meeting with a separist leader of India's Jammu-Kashmir Janab Abdul Ghani Lone. He just had returned from Azad Jammu-Kashmir after celebrating marriage ceremony of his son with the daughter of JKLF Chief Amanullah khan. Janab Abdul Ghani Lone had an opportunity to meet General Parwej Musharraf. He had intimated General regarding blood bath because of rising extremism in Pakistan. This extremis might cause irreparable loss in Pakistan, Lone saab had pointed to the General. Here I must say that it was the last interview of

Author along with an important leader and other dignitaries in Pakistan

Janab Abdul Ghani Lone, as he was shot dead at very near distance during a public meeting just after few days of this interview Islamabad was only political capital of Pakistan but it had also become working place of ISI, Army of Pakistan and other extremist groups. Extremists groups were being nourished by ISI and Pak army and were utilized against India. Islamabad was providing fearless environment to all extremist organizations. Extremists are stronger than anybody in Islamabad and an example of Lal Masjid is enough to understand their power. I will narrate the story of Lal Masjid later, first I want to tell you my entire experiences of Islamabad visit.

Though we had very busy schedule in Islamabad yet I wanted to meet some of extremist leaders. I was hundred percent sure about their presence in Islamabad. Actually I wanted to know their justification behind operating terrorist orGhanizations. I utilized my links and got hope to meet with Chief of Hijbul Mujahiddin Saiyed Salauddin.

I was expecting this would be meeting a highly success but it was not as easy as looked. I got information that Pir saab (Janab Syed was also called Pir sahab) would return Islamabad after two days, then only meeting would be possible. I became depressed and was thinking about ISI interference into my meeting with Pir saab. But suddenly I got massage that I must not leave hotel room. One of commander of Hijbul Mujahiddin was coming to see me. Now anxiously I was waiting for him. Commander of Hijbul Mujahiddin came along with his commander. I welcomed him and introduced myself. He said, I know everything about you, and ordered his commander to stay outside. He alone entered into my room. I had a brief talk with this Hijbul commander. We started talking about freedom movement in India's Jammu and Kashmir, then I asked about their relationship with separist leaders of India and

Jinna Super Market at Islamabad(famous for books)

An Encounter with Pakistan's Reality

I also wanted to know about their contribution and interference in the movement of freedom struggle. Hijbul Commander openly took the names of Indian Separist leaders and said that they could not run politics without theirs help. Hijbul help them in winning election and then forced them to place police officers and administrative officerson their desired places. It was a shocking fact for me and for every Indian. Hijbul Commander took the names of only those separist leaders who were active in India's Jammu-Kashmir. I clearly knew there that Separist leaders shout slogans against the interference of India and take help from terrorist orGhanizations. Actually Islamabad has been helping terrorist orGhanizations to create terror and tension in India's Jammu-Kashmir. OrGhanization like Hijbul Mujahidin gets fund from Islamabad and utilizes it in India's Jammu-Kashmir. Though Govt. of Pakistan denies this fact. Hijbul Commander honestly said that Pir Saab could not meet me because of urgent work & thus he had send him to meet me. Even the walls have ear and my meeting with one of Hijbul Commander did not remain secret. I found my journalist friends surprised and also worried because of this meeting. On the other hand I remained excited and curious. Coming to the city of Islamabad, I found it costliest city in Pakistan. Islamabad is a beautiful but costly city and a dream city for an average Pakistani citizen. Habitually I used to purchase news papers in every morning. In Pakistan and found it too costly. I think no any country of the world sells news papers as costly as Pakistan. In India, we get from local to national news paper in-between rupees 1 to 3,and in Pakistan it cost rupees 10 to 15. If we talk about magazines, an average magazine in Pakistan cost in-between rupees 100 to 150. For an average Pakistani , purchasing news papers or magazines is luxury. Our next destination was Muzaffarabad. Muzaffarabad is the capital city of Pakistan occupied Kashmir. It was a matter of pleasure for us that after visiting Mirpur Kotla region,again we were supposed to visit in that part of Kashmir where Indians are not allowed to visit. I started thinking about my next destination. Hotel staff informed me that it was going to be the most exciting journey. We had to reach Muzaffarabad from Islamabad through spiral roads on hilly way.

■■■

Chapter 23
Controversial Lal Masjid

Hard realities of Lal Masjid (Mosque) hammer more strongly into the minds than the beauty of Islamabad sooths into the hearts. It is a common belief that the places of worship are the places of God, whatever we name them either Allah, Ishwar, God or waheguru. As a human being, we go to places of worship only with pious reasons. At soul level we connect ourselves from almighty. But Lal Masjid is known for other reasons. It was become a place of less worship and more conspiracy. This Lal Masjid has become shelter of extremists, terrorists and Talibanis. Though people associated with the management of Lal Masjid always denied these realities and said it was all conspiracy to defame Lal Masjid.

We must know how historically Lal Masjid is important. It was constructed in 1965, during construction of Islamabad as the capital city of Pakistan. Red marbles were used

Famous Lal Masjid of Islamabad

in the interiors of this Mosque and finally it was popularly

Maulana Abdul Rashid Gazi

named Lal Masjid. This Lal Masjid came in existence with the existence of Islamabad as capital city and thus it is the oldest Mosque of Islamabad. The Central Development Corporation of Islamabad also considers Lal Masjid as the oldest Masjid of Islamabad.

People say that relationship between extremists and Lal Masjid is as old as the construction of Lal Masjid. Maulana Mohammad Abdullah was elected as the first Imam of this Lal Masjid in 1965. Maulana Mohammad Abdullah was known for his religious fundamentalism. He was extremist in nature. He was very close to the then dictator, President General Zia-ul-Haque. So since beginning, Lal Masjid remained a safe heaven for extremists and terrorists.

From 1979 to 1989, Imam Maulana Abdullah remained busy in giving armed training to newly recruited Mujahhidin to fight against Army of Russia in Afghanistan. We need not to say that it all was happening with the hundred percent support and initiatives of the ISI and army of Pakistan.

Strict rules are followed in Islamabad. No body can erect even a pillar without the permission of the Islamabad development corporation. Illegal construction is a big crime in Islamabad. These rules no where exist in the vicinity of Lal Masjid. A huge illegal construction has been constructed in the vicinity of Lal Masjid and it is fenced with high walls. It looks like covered fort rather than is the place of worship. Why Islamabad Development Corporation was helpless in taking actions against management of Lal Masjid?

We already have the answer. Lal Masjid get the patronage of the ISI, Pakistani army & Pakistani administration. Lal Masjid captures the land and opens Madarsa for women (Jamia Hafsa Madarsa) and men (Jamia Faridiya Madarsa). These Madarsas are used to crop more fundamentalists and extremists. They don't teach humanity and brotherhood. In 1998 Imam Maulana Mohammad Abdullah was killed and then two sons of Late Imam Md. Abdul Aziz Gazi and Mohammed Abdul Rashid Gazi took control on the administration of Lal Masjid. They went one step ahead than his father and converted Lal Masjid into armed training center for extremist, that in the course of time became big problem for even Government of Pakistan. Abdul Gazi and Rashid Gazi were recognized administrator of Lal Masjid so it was hard to make them step down from their posts. But both made a big blunder in 2005. They announced that whoever from Pakistan army was killed in the fight with Talibani Militant, must not be cremated with Islamic ritual. It was really a blunder and both the brothers were forced to step down.

ISI and Pakistani Army provide arms and funds to terrorist organizations. They have been treating Lal Masjid as one of organization engaged in cropping militants with their fund. It became clear when administration of Pakistan and Lal Masjid came in front of each other and clash together. It was obvious that Talibans started taking shelter inside Lal Masjid.

A few girls, who were student of Jamia Hafsa Madarsa complained against selling of unethical sex video tapes in the surround of Lal Masjid.. Boys of Jamia Faridiya Madarsa supported the cause of girl student. They kidnapped owner of a brothel and demanded to immediate ban on the sale of sex video tapes and immediate closure of all brothels.

But nothing could be done against brothel owners. It was believed that brothel owners had direct contact with top bureaucrates and even army officials. When no action was taken to close brothels, students took administration in their hand. They had support of both the brothers Abdul Gazi and Rashid Gazi and this support made them extremely powerful. They started behaving like Taliban and openly went against law of the nation. They did not hear repetitive calls by Pakistan police to free owner of brothel. At last police arrested two ladies who were teacher of Jamia Hafsa Madarsa. This action of Pakistan police broke fire and in the support of protestors, all the fundamentalist organization stopped the movement on the Islamabad roads. When police took action, they started pelting stones. Protestors kidnapped two police officers along with police jeep. Both the Chief of Lal Masjid Abdul Gazi and Rashid Gazi threatened to the Government of Pakistan for Jehad (war against Government) and then police was forced to release arrested women. The then President General Parwej Mushrraf had accepted regarding presence of Fiyadin Dasta (Terroriest) inside Lal Masjid. It was also accepted that Fiyadin Dasta was responsible for the attack on Marriot Hotel at Islamabad. It was the incidence of January 2007. After that Abdul Aziz and Rashid Aziz opened a Kazi court inside Lal Masjid and announced a three days religious conference. This step was like running a parallel government. Announcement from Lal Masjid had an impact and a huge crowd gathered to attended three days religious conference.

This big crowd gave a feel of power, success and a supermacy. To show the strength & power, the students and extremist went on the top of Lal Masjid and other buildings, and shouted slogans " Al Jehad, Al Jehad" just before Jume ki Namaj (Prayer of Friday). During the conference a shopkeeper came forward and surrendered all the unethical video tapes to destroy in front of gathered crowd. Then it was announced from Lal Masjid that whoever will come forward to destroy unethical video tapes, postures and other materials will be rewarded with fund to do other business and if any one will found not obeying the announcement will be punished according to Islamic law. Both the brothers gave a dead line of 30days to follow their order. People saw youth with guns and women covered with Burqua were shouting slogans against police and administration of Pakistan. It was decided to close all brothels and liquor shops within period of dead line. It worsen the situation. Extremists, terrorist, Fiyadin Dasta, whoever were inside Lal Masjid took guns in hand.Police was deputed to handle this situation. Police was outside the Lal masjid and extremist were inside the Lal Masjid. This gun battle took lives of twenty people counting students, protestors, businessmen and media people. At last Government of Pakistan had lodged FIR for murder, kidnapping and conspiracy against both the brothers Abul Gazi and Rashid Gazi. Followers of Lal Masjid were justifying their acts telling that they were fighting against owner of brothels and seller of unethical sex materials. They had nothing against government.

Fundamentalists were justifying their acts on the line of Islam. A peace talk was organized. Minister of religious affair Ejaul Haque and chairman of Muslim League Janab Chaudhary Sujat participated in peace talk with both the brothers. Abdul Gazi and Rashid Gazi both the brothers though accepted the points of compromise during talk but later rejected thoroughly. On 4 july 2007, the Government of Pakistan asked to all the protestors and students hidden inside Lal Masjid to surrender. Government also promised that the entire surrendered person will not be punished and will be given benefits in government plannings. Almost 1000 students came out from Lal Masjid and surrendered. Government of Pakistan sends army an officer disguised in Burqua inside Lal Masjid to talk with both the brothers. This army officer arrested one brother Abdul Gazi and then asked to surrender second brother Rashid Gazi but he denied. Abdul Gazi demanded safe passage with their follower and promised to hand over the administration of Lal Masjid to the Government of Pakistan. The demand of Abdul Gazi was given status of agreement and it was signed by Ulemas and top officials of Government of

Army Tank is being used to vacate Lal Mosque from hard core Militants

An Encounter with Pakistan's Reality

Pakistan and it happened with the consent of Prime Minister Shaukat Aziz and Chaudhary Sujat Hussain.

But President General Parwej Musharraf rejected this agreement and ordered an action against Rashid Gazi and his followers hidden inside Lal Masjid. Army started "operation silence". During this operation few hundred women were also inside Lal Masjid. Army along with police jointly carried this operation at mid night and successfully executed it. Many protestors surrendered. Approx 50 women and children along with the wife of Rashid Gazi were rescued in this operation and eight police officers were killed. At last 164 trained commanders of army & police together took complete control on Lal Masjid. Abdul Gazi did not surrender even after repeated calls. He was killed in operation. People also say that Abdul Gazi was killed by Taliban follower because he had made up his mind to surrender.

On this entire incidence , General Parwej Musharraf said on National Television that it was his bad luck that he had to fight against his own men, they had adopted a wrong way and became terrorist. They were defaming Islam and were fighting against Nation. We can not allow anyone to misuse the pious place like our Mosque. Our eight police officers have sacrificed their lives for the Nation.

It was the end of black chapter of Lal Masjid. But still no one can say Lal Masjid is out of extremist & fundamentalists. 18 police personnel and one citizen were killed in a bomb blast near this Lal Masjid on 6th July 2008.

■ ■ ■

Chapter 24

India's Most Wanted

Now I could able to understand the political Stunt of Govt. of Pakistan and the real feeling of common citizen of Pakistan.

It was the last day of our visit at Islamabad. Tomorrow on 25th November we had to move towards Muzaffarabad. In the mean time I met with a person whose name was enrolled in the list of India's most wanted . His name was Amanullah Khan.

Amanullah khan was a Pakistani citizen and a founder member of Jammu-Kashmir Liberation Front. His area of movement is spread from Rawalpindi-Islamabad o Muzaffarabad, Gilgit, and Batalistan. This separist leader had been raising his voice for the freedom of divided Kashmir of both the sides of Line of Control. He has been driving his movement even against Govt. of Pakistan and was imprisoned many times. To see him moving openly can put any one in surprise. Not only this Amanullah khan, but many others who are in the list of India's most wanted, openly move in Pakistan and fearlessly operate their gangs to spread terror in India. Under National & International pressure, sometimes Govt. of Pakistan arrests them but release them earliest. Stand of Pakistan on those India's most wanted never remained clear.

Pakistani Separatist leader Amanullah khan and his People

What they say they never implement. We all understand the double face of Pakistan.

Government of Pakistan always denies to have any connection with terrorist organizations like JKLF and on the otherhand ISI and Army of Pakistan have been helping various terrorist organizations with funds and various facilities like, providing space for training camps, weapons etc.

It was not an easy task to get Amanullah Khan for an interview. He was the man who started armed struggle In India's Kashmir in the name of freedom movement in 1988.

I was preparing questions that could be asked to Amanullah Khan. A meeting with him before leaving for Muzaffarabad was really important.

Before giving detail of conversation between myself and Amanullah khan, we must know the background of JKLF.

Md. Sheikh Abdullah, President of National Conference and Prime Minister & Chief Minister of India's Jammu Kashmir had created Jammu Kashmir Liberation Front

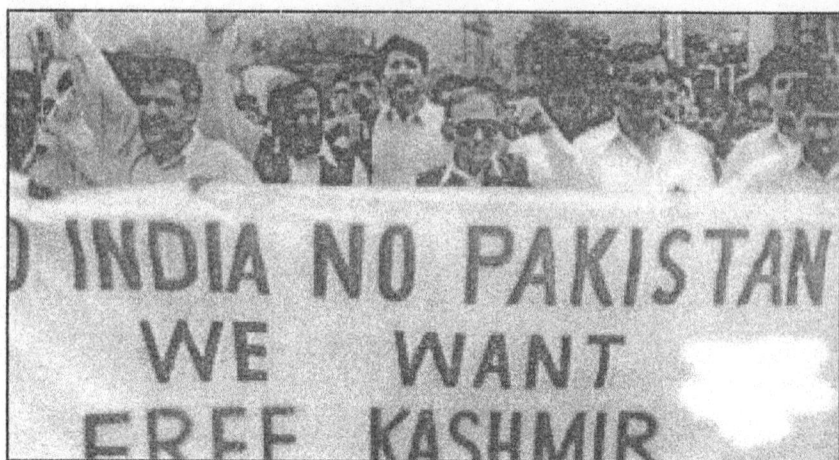
Separatist leader Amanullah Khan and his supporters shouting slogans for freedom from Pakistan

(JKLF) as one of wing of Janmat Sangrah Front. Most of the people attached with Janmat Sangrah Front were demanding for people's consensus to solve Kashmir problem .

JKLF was formally announced in Britain on May 1977. One of Founders of JKLF, Amanullah Khan along with with very few like minded people had started this organization. Earlier most of the active members of JKLF were either killed or arrested by India's Border Security Force. So Amanullah Khan was desperately looking for the youth who could join the JKLF. People who joined JKLF in Britain, had migrated people from Mirpur kotli region of Pakistan Occupied Kashmir. JKLF was spread in two parts. One JKLF started fighting for freedom of Azad Jammu-Kashmir and other JKLF started fighting for the freedom of India's Jammu-Kashmir. People say that JKLF is one organization with two branches.

In 1990 Yasin Malik was arrested as one of militant and was released after four years in 1994. Then Yasin Malik had announced that he would organize his separate JKLF and would operate armed struggle to achieve freedom of India's Jammu-Kashmir. Up to 1996 Indian army either had killed or arrested most of the militants of JKLF. Very few, who were survived, joined Shabbir Siddiqui to spread terror in India's Jammu-Kashmir.

A defeated Yasin Malik had changed his strategy and announced to continue peaceful movement for the freedom of Kashmir. JKLF has been trying to collect the public consensus from the people of Kashmir living across Line Of Control and instigating them to participate in freedom movement. All Party Hurriyat Conference became one of associates of JKLF.

In the decades of 70 & 80 JKLF was being operated from Pakistan Occupied Kashmir and London. Amanullah Khan and Hashmi Kuraishi were operating JKLF from London and Farukh Haider and Mohammed Mujafar from Pakistan occupied Kashmir.

People associated with JKLF have been spreading terror through their various acts. In 1971 an Indian Airlines was hi-jacked by the close associates of JKLF leaders Altaf and Hashim Kuraishi. Makbul Batt who had escaped from Indian jail in 1968, was master mind behind the hi-jack of Indian plane. In 1976 Makbul Batt returned back India and was arrested. In 1978 he was punished with death sentence. Makbul Batt also had killed a senior police officer.

On 3 Feb 1984, Ravindra Mhatre, an employee of Indian embassy at Barkingham was kidnapped by the JKLF people. JKLF wanted the release of Makbul Batt and thus had kidnapped Mhatre. Neither the JKLF nor the Government of India could reach on any final deal. JKLF people killed Mhatre on 6 February and Makbul Batt was hanged on 11 February in India.

After this incidence a new terrorist organization was formed by the Mhatre's kidnapper. It was named Kashmir

Liberation Army. The British Government filed a criminal case against Amanullah Khan for the killing of Mhatre. Though Amanullah Khan could not be convicted but was ordered to leave Britain. Amanullah Khan returned Pakistan. Here he established his relationships with the ISI and the Pakistani army and started working on the plan of opening training camps for militants in Pakistan Occupied Kashmir.

After 1987 election in the state of Jammu and Kashmir, some Kashmiri youth had crossed the line of control and joined the militant training camps. The JKLF had widened its network in entire Kashmir and with two blasts in Srinagar they created a situation of revolt.

Today JKLF wants a United Kashmir. Now they don't want people's vote, they want complete freedom. Neither they want to merge in India nor in Pakistan.

JKLF leaders also have different opinion on the status of Gilgit and Batalistan. Few considers this part already merged in Pakistan and few considers it still a part of undivided Kashmir. Actually few separist leaders speak the language of ISI and PAK army. Whoever speak against Govt. of Pakistan, faces strong reaction of ISI & Pak army. As for example, when Makbul Batt reached Pakistan in 1968 after escaping from Indian jail, he was arrested there and was put in jail for few months.

Analysts say that apart from all the differences between ISI and JKLF, ISI is dependent on JKLF to create terror in India's Jammu-Kashmir.

JKLF helps ISI in spreading terror and in recruiting militants for training. And in response ISI provides funds to JKLF . ISI could able to established terrorist organization like Hijbul Mujahiddin, Harkat-ul-Ansar, Lashkar-e-taiba etc with the great help of JKLF. Pakistan acts like big brother for the terrorist organizations written above. Pakistan provides funds and arms to them and keep them under its influence.

On 11 & 12 Feb 1998 ISI and army of Pakistan had forcefully closed the militant training camps which were being operated by the JKLF in the Mirpur Kotli region. The ISI also remained pioneer in killing of two JKLF leaders on 13th July 1997 at a Muzaffarabad. It all was clear indication for JKLF leaders that they must obey ISI.

According to analyst on Kashmir issue JKLF has been weakened. Yasin Malk drives his own JKLF because of conflict with other JKLF leaders. JKLF headed by Amanullah Khan and lost its influence in India when Shabbir Siddiqui along with 37 supporter of JKLF were killed in two different encounter in Hajratbal in 1996. 11 militants of JKLF were killed on 24th march 1996 and 26 militants including Shabbir Siddiqui were killed on 29 march 1996.

At present Amanullah Khan operates JKLF in POK.

He along with dozens of JKLF militant had tried thrice to cross line of control but was badly defeated by Pak army & Indian Border Security Force (BSF).

■■■

Chapter 25

Amanullah Khan Raises Voice to Get Back China-occupied Land

My meeting with founder and chairman of JKLF was very important. Amanullah khan lives in muzaffarabad, an important city of Pakistan occupied Kashmir. When I met him, he was looking older. Amanullah khan showed his satisfaction on the initiatives taken by both the nations India and Pakistan to solve Kashmir problem. He was the man who started armed struggle for the freedom of Kashmir and now was talking about peaceful means to solve Kashmir issue. He was completely against with the formula given by General Parwej Musharraf to divide undivided Kashmir into seven parts.

Amanullah khan had been raising his voice for the complete freedom of undivided kashmir. He had been dreaming a free Kashmir that was in existence before 1947. Amanullah khan strongly put his voice against existence of army in both the parts of Kashmir.

He says, India & Pakistan both must get back their army first and then they can reach on certain solution.

Undivided Kashmir will be free country with very good relationship with both the countries India & Pakistan.

It will be responsibility of free & sovereign kashmir that it must not allow any nation to misuse its land under any influence. India and Pakistan also have to promise that they will not interfere into the internal matter of independent Kashmir.

Amanullah khan straight forward said that he not only wanted freedom from India & Pakistan but also deserved to get back china occupied land, that Pakistan delivered to China.

It is just for your information that this Amanullah Khan was listed amongst India's ten most wanted terrorist living in Pakistan. This Amanullah khan also said :- If Kashmir is being

King of undivided Kashmir,
Maharaja Hari Singh

liberated, then it must remain under protection of United Nations for at least Fifteen years and all the elections must be conducted under surveillance of United Nations. This is the only alternative to tackle the influence of India & Pakistan. Only people of Kashmir should be given right to take decision regarding their preferences to merge either with India or Pakistan or remain independent.

Since 1947 Kashmir remain sole issue in all the Indo-Pak wars and in all the terrorist activities in India. It is essential to find out the roots of Kashmir problem. I wanted Amanullah's point of view on this question. Amanullah khan answered in detail :- Britishers took control India by taking control on almost 565 small and big estates running in that period. Though all the estates were being ruled by Zamindars or Maharaja (King) but actually all were slave of British administration.

In 1947 it had been decided that India will get independence with the partition and a new country Pakistan will come in existence. In this circumstances all the estates were given freedom to choose the nation, they wanted to merge.

King of Kashmir Maharaja Hari Singh was confused on this issue. He was Hindu king and Muslim population was in majority in his kingdom. New nation Pakistan was being created on the basis of religion. Supporters of Pakistan wanted to merge in Pakistan because of their religion. So in the month of October 1957, Kabailis attacked on Jammu-Kashmir to merge in Pakistan. Maharaja Hari Singh took help of Indian army with the promise to merge in India. This decision of Maharaja Hari Singh created a lot of controversies. India had clear-cut stand. Maharaja Hari Singh had showed his willingness to merge in India . After signing on agreement India had send his army to counter Kabailis attacker. Pakistan had been giving plea that India took signature of Maharaja Hari Singh under pressure. When Indian army entered in Kashmir illegally, Maharaja was forced to sign an agreement regarding merging in India.

This aspects remained unending controversies in-between India & Pakistan.

Answer of Amanullah Khan was almost correct. Pakistan still have control on one-third part of Kashmir. Though India has been showing its protest loudly since 1947. This part of Kashmir has been bleeding continuously. China still has control over illegally transferred Kashmiri land by Pakistan. This land is called Oxychin.

Whatever the most of population of Pakistan Occupied Kashmir are fed up with the violence. Whoever earlier wanted to merge in Pakistan, now wanted to get free as an independent state. They denied any merger with either nation and dream to achieve free undivided Kashmir.

Further Amanullah Khan said that terrorist organizations like the Lashkar-e-taiba, Jaish-e-mohammed, Alkaida have changed the meaning of armed struggle for freedom, that he had started in Jammu-Kashmir. They have hijacked the concept of freedom struggle, said Khan.

I was seeing a changed Amanullah khan. He was almost talking about peaceful ways to achieve solution of Kashmir problem.

Amanullah khan looked carrying various differences at thought level with JKLF chief Yasin Malik and with leaders of Hurriyat conference. Amanullah khan was demanding complete freedom of entire undivided Kashmir and Yasin malik has been demanding freedom for only India's Jammu-Kashmir.

Amanullah khan was considering terrorist and conspirator Maqbul Batt as hero. Makbul bhatt was hanged in India.

Amanulla khan showed his extreme wish & will to solve Kashmir issue with peaceful means. He criticized army of Pakistan who killed eight of his supporters while he was crossing line of control to enter into Indian territory.

Jammu-Kashmir is the land of those people who are breathing there since thousands of years and no any decision could be taken without their wish & will added Amanullah answering my question.

JKLF chief Amanullah khan revealing his opinion on Laddakh Said: "If people of Laddakh want to go separate they must be allowed. Pointing on Kashmir problem he said that 40 percent of Kashmir problems continues to exist because of leaders of Kashmir, 30 percent because of India's leadership, 20 percent because of PAK leadership and 10 percent because of international community. Separist leaders like Prof. Abdul Gani Batt and Syed Shah Gilani have made Kashmir issue complicated. Leaders of international communities got confused when they see various opinions of various leaders on the same problem Kashmir. Amanullah khan looked depressed because of different opinions of different leaders.

I straight forward asked a question to him : Don't you feel you are also responsible for the present situation in Kashmir".

Amanullah khan replied 'yes'. He also accepted that few freedom fighters (terrorist) disobeyed rules and regulation formulated by him and killed the pundits of this valley. It was resulted into mass migration of Kashmir Hindu. Migration of pundits from Kashmir remained the most sad part of freedom struggle of Kashmir. He also said that migrated pundits must be called back.

His dream to achieve freedom with armed struggle was totally scattered. Amanullah khan accepted this fact indirectly. His armed struggle took turn and became religious war and it was a biggest disaster. It killed the secular image of Kashmir.

Here I want to unfold a fact that daughter of Amanullah khan was married with the son of Kashmiri separist leader Abdul Ghani Lone.

I had interviewed Abdul Ghani Lone at his residence at Jammu-Kashmir when he just had returned from Pakistan Occupied Kashmir after attaining the marriage function of his son with the daughter of Amanullah khan. In interview Janab Lone has said that he got an opportunity to meet General Parwej and had requested him not to trust on Laskhars(militant organization) otherwise they could back fire to kill him. After this interview janab Lone was killed in the hand of terrorists. After few days of this incidence, General Parwej Musharraf was also attacked by some terrorists. I was simply recalling words of Late Abdul Ghani Lone.

After interviewing Amanullah khan I packed my luggage as fast as possible. We had to move towards Muzaffarabad. We took seats inside a mini bus. I was excited. I had seen Mirpur Kotli region of POK and now was visiting muzaffarabad an another city of POK. I already had information regarding some armed training camps running in the city of muzaffarabad. ISI, Pak Army and Pak Government all support these militant training camps to spread terror in India's Kashmir.

Interview with Amanullah had cleared the approach of a separist leader on Kashmir and I was considering it as an achievement of this tour.

■■■

Chapter 26
Kohala, Where Pandit Nehru Was Detained

We took breakfast in Holiday Inn hotel and said good bye to Islamabad. We were moving towards Muzaffarabad. It was a journey of 5 to 6 hours by bus. Grand wide roads of Islamabad was left behind and our mini bus was passing through spiral hilly roads. Media persons of both the nations felt closer in this journey and started sharing their emotions. The personal experiences of one of our Pakistan journalist friend put us in great shock.

According to him one day in Islamabad he was returning from his bank after withdrawing some

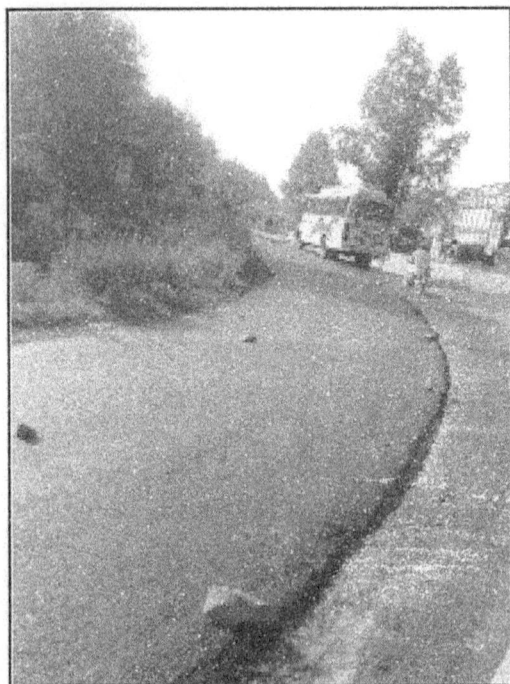

Kohala Islamabad- Muzaffarabad Road

money. He was counting his money while walking on the road. Suddenly a few people caught him from behind and took him in the office of ISI. He was badly beaten there. The ISI put allegation on him that Indian High Commission had given him that money for spying against Pakistan. Our Pakistan journalist friend showed them the bank paper of withdrawal of money but they did not accept any proof. He was confined into criminal cell of ISI and was released after many days when journalist friends started writing against this incidents and the ISI. This incident was really shocking for me. The ISI could torture even honorable citizen & journalist of the nation. After listening the story of the Pakistani journalist friend we all became serious. Breaking the seriousness of the situation, an another Pakistani journalist friend informed that we were about to reach Moori hill station. This hill station was developed by British administration. In summer entire administration of state of Punjab shift at Moori hill station just like entire administration of Jammu-Kashmir shift in Srinagar in summer. I took my head out of window and started seeing magical natural beauty of Moor hill station. I was also told that before partition, The Indians used this way to enter into Kashmir. At that time Tanga (Horse Rikshaw) was only transport. We did not had any plan to stay at Moori hills. Our minibus was passing through the spiral roots of Moori hills and I was passionately looking at bungalows made by the British in the lap of immense natural beauty. There I was informed that Moori hill station is a tourist hill place of Pakistan and remains crowded throughout the year. It was a visual treat to see Moori hills even while aboard by a bus.

Enjoying the ultimate natural beauty on the way, we reached at Kohala. Kohala is a small place in between Islamabad & Muzaffarabad. Our bus stopped there for a breakfast. I wanted to know little bit more about kohala. I

Author Satish Verma at Kohala Road

was aware with the historical importance of kohala. Actually when Maharaja Hari Singh were in power, he had arrested Pt. Nehru and confined him here in kohala. When Labor party of England showed his desire to free India but only after partition and creation of a new nation Pakistan, then people of Muslim league started campaigning to take Kashmiri Muslim in favor of Pakistan. National conference the then was Muslim conference were opposing the move of Muslim league considering them outsider. They were just creating controversy. Md. Ali Jinna, leader of Muslim league had visited Kashmir in 1945. People of Kashmir protested against him and did not give any importance. Leader of Muslim Conference smelled some conspiracy in the visit of Md. Ali Jina. It was the time when people of Kashmir started showing their preference for India.

Seeing all the above situation Sheikh Abdullah started a movement and gave slogan " quit Kashmir". He started putting pressure on Dogra king to step down. Complete slogan was " Break the Amritsar agreement and quit

Kashmir" (Bainama Amritsar tod do, Kashmir chhod do). Actually it was a movement to divide Kashmir into two parts. This undivided Kashmir had been kept safe because of wisdom king Gulab Singh and with sacrifice of 30,000 Dogra soldiers.

Actually Jammu-Kashmir was established on the basis of Amritsar accord. But the "quit Kashmir" movement of Sheikh Abdullah had become of great danger for the existence of Jammu and Kashmir. Some historians say that Sheikh Abdullah and Pandit Nehru were good friend to each other and under influence of friendship Pt. Nehru were supporting Sheikh Abdullah`s "Quit Kashmir" movement. In 1946 "quit India movement" was on peak and in Kashmir "quit Kashmir movement" were getting fire. The then Prime Minister of Kashmir Pt. Ram Chandra Kak ordered to arrest Sheikh Abdullah and his important associates to freeze "quit Kashmir movement". Sheikh Abdullah with his associates were arrested and put into the Srinagar jail.

Pt. Nehru was considered to be the Prime-Minister of independent India. He decided to visit the Srinagar jail to meet his friend Sheikh Abdullah. Pandit Nehru decided to reach Srinagar by road.

Pandit Nehru reached uninterrupted up to Muzaffarabad district but was arrested on kohla bridge by the order of the then Prime Minister Pandit Ramchander Kak. Though Pandit

Kohala, Witness of the friendship of Sheikh Abdullah and Pandit Nehru

Nehru had threatened Pandit Ramchander Kak that he would teach him a lesson. Pandit Ramchander Kak remained unfazed. Within few hours lady mountbaiten got news that Pandit Nehru was arrested in Kashmir. Lady Mountbaiten was considered a good friend of Pandit Nehru. She requested King Hari Singh to release Pandit Nehru. Hari Singh honored the request of Lady Mountbaiten and ordered to release Pandit Nehru. Pandit Nehru returned back Delhi. In Delhi Pandit. Nehru convinced Mahatama Gandhi that Prime Minister of Kashmir Pandit Ramchander Kak must step down from his post. Maharaja Hari Singh was pressurized by Mahatma Gandhi to remove Pt. Ramchander Kak from the post of Prime-Minister. Pandit Kak was removed from his chair and this way Pandit Nehru successfully took his revenge.

Prof. Bhim Singh, an analyst of Jammu-Kashmir affairs, has written all the above facts in his book, " Jammu & Kashmi, the blunders and way out". Actually Maharaja Hari Singh was totally against of partition of Jammu-Kashmir and he found Pt. Nehru a good friend to Sheikh Abdullah, so he started seeing Pt. Nehru as an enemy of Kashmir. This was the time when top political leaders under the influence of British ruler, were preparing division of India and Kashmir on the basis of religion. Whatever, we reached Kohala and was surprised to see the displayed banners and posters demanding freedom of Jammu & Kashmir. People of Jammu-Kashmir Libration Front were informed earlier about the arrival of media people and thus they had already displayed banner & posters reflecting demands. When we reached there, they started shouting slogans. They wanted to get their voice heard by Indian Government and Pakistan Government simultaneously. They were fighting for complete freedom and did not want any interference ,even interference of Government of Pakistan.

Actually people of the JKLF avail every possible opportunity to loud their voice and it was a big opportunity for them. Protester were keen to meet us, they wanted to reveal their emotion to us but they were not allowed to have direct interaction with media people. I was thinking to see that historical guest house where Pt. Nehru were detained. I could not able to see that historical guest house. We were in group and just had stopped there for having some snacks & breakfast.

After finishing breakfast our journey started again. We were about to reach Muzaffarabad. Earlier people used cover the distance from Lahore to Rawalpindi and up to Srinagar from horse cart (Tanga). I was thinking about danger and excitement of that journey. We reached Muzaffarabad. It was a great journey. We were into the lap of nature. Muzaffarabad was situated on the bank of Neelam and Jhelum river. The moment we stepped down from bus, we felt that we were in the most beautiful city. We were taken in hotel . We were almost tired but could not afford to have rest. We had to reach assembly of Muzaffarabad to meet some Kashmiri leaders. An interexchange of thought program was fixed on the issues like Indo-Pak relationship & freedom of Kashmir etc. We all media person were excited to attained scheduled program at Muzaffarabad. I was looking for an opportunity to see militant training camps. I was conscious about the presence of ISI. I was getting ready to reach assembly of Muzaffarabad.

■ ■ ■

Chapter 27

Muzaffarabad: A City of Ultimate Natural Beauty

No doubt India's Jammu-Kashmir is known as heaven on Earth but natural beauty of Pakistan occupied Azad Jammu-Kashmir is nothing less. Actually nature has poured its beauty on entire undivided Kashmir but rulers and politicians have divided Kashmir in parts.

Muzaffarabad, Capital City of Azad Jammu and Kashmir

Politicians have created borders. Muzaffarabad is the capital city of Pakistan occupied Azad Jammu-Kashmir. Nature has blessed this city with its immense beauty. This city is the combination of valley and hills and is situated on the bank of Jhelum & Neelam river. Actually both the rivers dissolve into one another at one place in Muzaffarabad. Muzaffarabad is spread in 6117sq. kilometer and nourishes a population of approx eight lakh people. Still today most of the residence of Pakistan occupied Kashmir blame Dogra ruler for doing agreement with Indian government for the merger in India. The agreement was signed in 1947. Citizens of Azad Jammu-Kashmir believed that they could not able to achieve freedom from Pakistan because of this misdeed of Dogra ruler.

Broder of Azad Jammu-Kashmir touches Pakistan from east, geographically it looks like moon from top angle. It is 600 Kilometers long and 15 to 60 kilometers in wide. On the map it looks half moon shaped. One side of Azad Jammu and Kashmir is plane area of Mirpur region

Reflecting beauty of Muzaffarabad, a hotel on the bank of lake

and on the otherside there is a chain of Himalayas hills. Here most of the hills are approx 6000 feet above the sea level. Jhelum, Neelam and Punch,all three rivers cross the land of Azad Jammu-Kashmir. These rivers create many small water drainage across hills and plane., River, plane, hills, forests all meet together in Azad Jammu-Kashmir and create ultimate natural beauty. It also touches western border of Pakistan and bifurcated by Indo-Pak line of control in the east.

Bagh, Bhimbhar, Mirpur-Kotli, Muzaffarabad, Punch and Sughunti are six districts of Azad Jammu-Kashmir. Muzaffarabad is a hilly city and famous for its tourist resorts. It is also a political center. You can get all kinds of tasty vegetarian and non-vegetarian foods in the market of muzaffarabad.

At the distance of 32 kilometer from Muzaffarabad, there is a pious shrine of Saint Pir Chinasi.

This shrine is encircled with hills and forest. If you are natural lovers, you will stuck to this place. Famous Neelam valley is situated in the north & north-east of Muzaffarabad. This valley is approximate 200 kilometer long and looks like running parallel to Kangan valley. Snow covered Himalayan hills bifurcate both the valley. Famous Jhelum river floats from east to west through these hills.

A beautiful small place Ghari Dupatta is situated at the distance of 24 kilometers from Muzaffarabad and a block Chaukati is situated at the distance of 35 Kilometers.

■■■

Chapter 28
Exchange of Thoughts

We reached Muzaffarabad from Islamabad in evening. We had to meet with political leaders and local members of legislative assembly in the premises of legislative assembly. Actually our all the movements was properly scheduled and we had to move according to given schedule.

Legislative Assembly of Azad Jammu and Kashmir

Secretary of Legislative assembly of Muzaffarabad interacting with Indian Journalists

We all media people were taken to muzaffarabad assembly. Continuation of Indo-Pak dialogue was a welcome step for all.

Muzaffarabad always has remained in news for carrying various armed training camps for militants. Offices of various terrorist groups exist there. Apart from this fact leaders of Muzaffarabad were showing positive gesture for Indo-Pak peace dialogues. Though I found clear cut differences on the formula given by General parwej Musharraf to divided Kashmir in seven parts.

Speaker of Muzaffarabad legislative assembly Sardar Mohammed Syab Khalid very politely side tracked the opinion of General on Kashmir. Sardar Syab were in favor of continuous peace process between India & Pakistan. It was the first time when the political leaders and media people of both the Nations were feeling closer. Only positive dialogues could fetch the positive result, Sardar

An Encounter with Pakistan's Reality

Syab put his strong view. When we put question related to armed struggle and terrorism in Kashmir, Sardar syab sahib replied very diplomatically. According to him, Mujahiddins were getting only moral and diplomatic help from them. They never helped them with arms and funds. He strongly denied about existence of any armed militant camp in Muzaffarabad.

Another Ministers like Masood Chaudhary and Minister for archaeological department Mufti Munsif also supported his statement.

We asked another question – "When 'Indo-Pak' peace dialogues are in progress, then armed struggle must be stopped immediately. Do you accept this? They said 'yes'. Peace process must given a chance and armed struggle must be stopped. Sardar Syab answered all my questions but he remained very diplomatic on the General's formula to divide Kashmir in seven parts. We also met with a very senior leader Sardar khan bahadur khan, he remained Minister continuous for the three terms and was still active in politics. He also supported the statement of speaker Sardar Syab. He also said that people of Azad Jammu-Kashmir is divided into parts. The majority of the people want to see Azad Jammu-Kashmir merged in Pakistan. We also have good number of people who want complete freedom, freedom from India and Pakistan both.

Apart from all these issue based conversation, we found everybody welcoming us and were happy to see ongoing Indo-
Pak peace process. We also discussed on Hindu religious place Sharda Pith. It was in really worst condition. Leaders of Muzaffarabad promised us that they would provide an opportunity for all Kashmiri pundits to visit Sharda Pith to satisfy their religious urge.

■■■

Chapter 29
Historical Temple of Goddess Sharda

I discussed about Temple of Goddess Sharda in previous chapter but in very short. Now I feel it is essential to give description of this temple in detail. There are two hill tops in Muzaffarabad named as Shardiya and Nardiya and there is a valley in-between these two top hills known as Sharda Valley.

Temple of Goddess Sharda on the hills of Muzaffarabad

People say that in ancient times a queen blessed with divine qualities had her kingdom here. The name of the queen was sharda. In the course of time this valley was named on her name and became famous as "Sharda Valley". History have some very authentic documentation about this Sharda Temple.

It was a famous center for religious study, Meditation and worship for all Kashmiri Pundits. Goddess Sharda temple once was so famous that this place was called "Sharda Desh" (A state of Goddess Sharda). People say that great Shankaracharya was honoured with " SARVYA JANYA PITHADHISH" at the temple of Goddess Sharda. Scholar & wise men Kashmiri pundits here used to teach Sanskrit language thinking it a service to the mankind. Shwetamber Jain Scholar had submitted here his research work to develop a grammar.

This fact is documented in historical jain manuscript 1277-78. It is known as "Prabhav Kritya". It was also in document that this Sharda Pith was also an education center for the followers of Buddhism. Here Sharda lipi and Takri lipi had been developed that helped in the evolution of today's Gurumukhi lipi. It is also said that famous Vaishnav saint Swami Ramunj had visited this place during his Sri Angam journey to study a great epic "Brahamashtra". Brahamasatra was preserved here. Swami Ramanuj studied "Brahamasutra" and written its analysis " with the name of "Brahamasatra Sribhasya"

It is said that statue of Goddess Sharda, established inside Shrengeri Sharda dham originally is made of pure Chandan wood. This statue of Goddess Sharda was earlier established here in Sharda pith and was taken to Shringeri Sharda Dham Mandir by the great Shankaracharya.

It was also documented in ancient epics that followers of King Gonda of Bengal, had been visiting Sharda pith to workship Goddess Sharda. First founder King of Kashmir, Maharaja Gulab Singh had renovated this Temple during his period and after that this Sharda temple had not been renovated till today. Kashmiri pundits has been continuously demanding the renovation of this temple. It is a matter of surprise that this Sharda Temple even is not in the list of tourist place of Pakistan Occupied Kashmir.

■■■

Chapter 30
Conspiracy of Pakistan

After interaction program at Muzaffarabad assembly, we were taken at the resident of the then Prime-Minister of Pakistan occupied Azad Jammu-Kashmir Janab Sardar Sikandar Hyat for dinner. There we had an opportunity to interact with honorable Prime Minister. It was well known fact that few people of Azad Jammu-Kashmir support the arms struggle for freedom in India's Jammu-Kashmir and even in POK few people have been demanding freedom of POK from Pakistan. People who have been rising voice for freedom also demanding people's vote for consensus. Putting these facts in front of Prime-minister, I asked his opinion? Prime Minister straight forward answered that the would vote in favor of Pakistan, even at cost of leaving Azad Jammu-Kashmir.

The statement of Prime Minister had showed the hard reality behind all the terrorism and armed struggle in both the parts of undivided Kashmir.

The then Prime Minister of Azad Jammu and Kashmir Sardar Sikander Hyat Khan

Prime Minister Sardar Siknadar Hyat showed his full faith in General Parwej Musharraf and supported his formula to divide Jammu-Kashmir in seven parts.

He also showed gratefulness towards the Government of Pakistan for giving economical assistance and made us sure about non-existence of any kind of militant training camp in Azad Jammu-Kashmir.

Citizens were living in completely peaceful environment. Other ministers also tried to convince us that every citizen of Azad Jammu-Kashmir had been enjoying total political freedom. They were supporting ongoing Indo-Pak peace process. They were almost fooling us. At last I put question to them. Why every citizen of Pakistan Occupied Kashmir has to fill a form before casting his/her vote during election that he/she accepts merger of Azad Jammu-Kashmir in Pakistan.

Leaders of the JKLF have been raising their voice against this atrocity. The Prime Minister could not answer for few seconds then he said, he will order to withdraw this rule. Now no body has to fill form before casting vote. It was just a promise not be fulfilled ever.

My next question was about demand of freedom from Pakistan by the people living in Pakistan Occupied Azad Jammu and Kashmir. To this, the PM replied in a very different way. He said that if people were given an opportunity to vote, they would vote in favour of Pakistan and if result would be different, I would like to leave Azad Jammu and Kashmir and would settle in Pakistan.

Further he said in excitement that in next coming election, he would like to invite Indian media to cover the entire election procedure.

We put another question: Don't you think that for solving the Kashmir problem, the leaders of Kashmir must be given importance and should be called in all the Indo-Pakistani dialogues.

The PM replied: If Kashmiri leaders will get an opportunity to share a space in-between Indo-Pak dialogues, then I will certainly call former Chief Minister of India's Jammu-kashmir Mufti MohammedSyed, Dr. Farookh Abdullah and other active leaders. P.M. Sikandar Hyat Khan informed us that about 30 lakh people live in Azad Jammu-Kashmir, in which 10 lakh have come from India's Jammu-Kashmir. One of Indian journalist asked: "Indo-Pak peace talk have become continuous process, still people are not leaving armed struggle"

P.M. answered : Nothing is happening on my direction or under my supervision. When people will get confidence that a certain solution will come in their way, they will leave arms.

P.M. of POK Sikandar Hyat Khan appreciated efforts of Prime-Minister of India Manmohan Singh, former Prime Minister Atal Bihari Bajpayee, President of Pakistan General Parwej Musharraf for keeping Indo-Pak peace talk a continuous process.

Dinner was fabulous. I found all the dishes well served and really tasty. But one thing was clearly visible. Entire administration of Pakistan occupied Azad Jammu-Kashmir were working under pressure Govt. of Pakistan ISI and Pak Army.

After dinner, we returned back to Sangam hotel, where we had been given accommodation. We had very busy schedule for tomorrow. People from Gilgit, Batlistan and from Sakurd tribal area, were supposed to come to meet us. Though it was not in the agenda made earlier.

■■■

Chapter 31
Chakauti Chauki of Pakistan

I was informed that tomorrow, in the early morning, we had to visit chakauti, the front army post of Pakistan near Indo-Pakistan line of control. I was really excited. Our stay at Muzaffarabad was very important from various angles.

Earlier I had to collect news about the happening or mishappening on the line of control but this time I was visiting every place and was becoming witness of every move. For me it was like a dream to see frontline Army Post Chakauti Chauki near line of control. It was a dream like situation and I was dreaming every bit of it.

Next morning, on 26th November, I got ready earlier than expected. I met some of the local people and found all of them happy to see Indo-Pakistani peace process at all possible level.

26th November was also the first annual day of cease fire on the line of control between India and Pakistan. A complete year had passed without firing on the line of control from either side.

A mini bus was arranged to carry us from Muzaffarabad to chakauti chauki. Mini bus was always preferred to travel through spiral hilly roads. It was a pleasant weather and we all were fascinated to see the natural beauty, which were passing with the speed of mini bus.

This is the first time after 1947, When media people from India were invited to visit Pakistan and to see even those places which were under tight security.

Our mini bus was running on Muzaffarabad -Srinagar road. Before partition this road had enough life. Major General of Inter-State Service , Major General Shaukat Sultan were our guide in this journey.

we reached Chaukati enjoying the pleasant weather and natural beauty of Muzaffarabad. Chaukati was situated on Muzaffarabad Srinagar road. There we saw a bridge dividing India and Pakistan. It was in worst condition. It was almost impossible to cross this bridge with army vehicle or even by a car. I attracted the attention of General Shaukat towards bridge and asked : How proposed Muzaffarabad-Srinagar bus service could be started. Major General Shaukat replied in full confidence " Janab let this bus service sanctioned by Indo-Pakistani administration; army of Pakistan and India will make this bridge perfectly fit within 24 hours". I must inform you that this bridge divides India and Pakistan on the line of control. From Muzaffarabad, you will have to walk only 10 kilometers on this road to reach Srinagar.

During conversation I came to know that Major General Shaukat Sultan had one more tag. He was also security advisor to President General Parwej Mushrraf. Major General Shaukat repeated many times that for all the mishappening and disaster on and surround of linc of control, only Indian army was responsible.

Major General Shaukat took us on line of control and said that, there was nothing like line of control.

One can identify line of control by seeing drainage and forests. Some drainage had height of eighty feet and some where less than one feet. Major General pointed at barren land and said these land were barren because of Indian

A scene of line of control at Chikauti Chawki

army. Actually he was directly blaming Indian army for unnecessary firing and uprooting the population once peacefully settled in that area. The Major General were putting allegations on Indian army and I was getting angry from deep of my heart and mind. Maor General Shaukat talked about a data that almost 35 thousands people from India 's Kashmir had migrated in Azad Jammu and Kashmir since 1988 and this process was still going on. He also critised for the fencing of line of control by Indian army, as it was against "Karanchi agreement". According to this agreement no any structure could be erected on line of control for defense purposes.

I found no body reacting from our side. I was loosing my patience. At last I reacted and replied Major with cool voice : Sir you said about these barren land and blamed on Indian army but had you ever thought what happened in India's Kashmir? Then I informed him that almost 2.5lakh Kashmiri pundits had to leave their motherland because of well planned firing and bombing by the Pakistan army from line of control.

People living in Kathua village to punch to Rajauri, had to vacate their villages to save their lives from the firing of Pakistan army. I attracted attention of Major General Shaukat on the killing of 5 innocent Gujjar Muslims because of blind firing of Pakistani army from line of control in R.S. pura area near line of control.

This cruel incident took place in village of Abduliya. I concluded my words telling him " Sir firing kills people and never differentiate between Hindu and Muslim. I thought Major General will reject my point of view but surprisingly he said " I see, I will confirm these incidence from my Army officers"

Major General appreciates Indo-Pakistani peace talks and interexchange of thought through media and intellectuals and showed his faith that these processes could solve Kashmir problem. We also had interaction with Jawan (Army constable) Ajmat Ulha. He revealed his feeling that after seize fire between India and Pakistan, they were living a better life and could move in open air otherwise we had to live inside Bunker only.

I was thinking that what could be seen more at line of control. The ISI and Pakistani army had continuous vigil on us and they took us back just after few moments telling us that there was nothing to see more. While we were returning back, bus stopped at chakauti block. I was surprised to see selling of CD, DVD and Video cassettes of Bollywood films at the shops of this small place Chakauti. The then Shahrukh khan starrer film Veer Jaara was in great demand. I was told that people of Azad Jammu and Kashmir were in love with Bollywood Films. We returned back Muzaffarabad. There I met with some of local people. All welcomed us and reflected their mind set. All wanted complete freedom and immediate opening of Srinagar-Muzaffarabad road. We also had an opportunity to interact with the member of Yasin Malik's JKLF. They were not ready for any further division of Jammu and Kashmir. Mohammed Siraduddin, a JKLF official was also in favour of opening of Srinagar-Muzaffarabad Road. He unfolded his emotion telling that it would be inhuman to stop any one from meeting their family members and close ones."

Md. Siraduddin appealed to both the nations, India and Pakistan to release all political prisoners from jail and both the nations must withdraw their army from Jammu and Kashmir. Mohammed Siraduddin accepted that armed struggle to achieve freedom was a wrong decision of JKLF and now they had stopped any kind of violence and started campaigning for freedom with peaceful meaning.

At Muzaffarabad we saw JKLF clearly divided into two parts. One group had come forward to welcome us and other group were shouting slogan against our presence in "Azad Jammu and Kashmir. In evening we returned to Hotel Sangam. We clearly observed differences in opinion regarding freedom of Jammu and Kashmir and its merger with Pakistan. All the political fraternity of Pakistan occupied Jammu and Kashmir were in favour of Pakistan Occupied Kashmir's merger with Pakistan and people of this region were demanding complete freedom. They were totally against merger either in Pakistan or India. Concept of freedom were different for different people. Whatever, we were utilizing and enjoying every move in Muzaffarabad and never forgot to justify our visit as an Indian journalist.

■■■

Chapter 32

Formula of Dividing Kashmir into Seven Parts

Every move of Muzaffarabad visit was proving happening one. We were getting new experiences after each interaction with one after another people. Few experiences were ultimate that we never had imagined earlier. In the morning of 27th November we were ready to see new places at Muzaffarabad. In the mean time again

Azad Jammu and Kashmir University

we got an opportunity to meet founder and chairman of JKLF Amanullah Khan. This time we had an interaction on serious issues affecting Indo-Pakistani relationship and Kashmir problem with him.

According to our schedule we had to visit Azad Jammu and Kashmir University and had to share our opinions on Kashmir issues with students and professors of the University. But when we reached University , saw student were discussing on the formula given by General Parwej Musharraf regarding division of Kashmir into seven parts.

We saw hot discussion between original habitant of Kashmir valley and other Kashmiri students. Hot discussion raised controversy and divided students in two groups. Actually National Student Federation(NSF) were shouting for complete freedom of Kashmir. NSF were supporters of JKLF. The other group were member of Muslim Student Federation(MSF). Students of MSF were supporter of Government of Pakistan running in Pak Occupied Jammu and Kashmir. When we reached here found very tense situation.

JKLF supporters (NSF) were shouting slogans for complete freedom of Kashmir and students of MSF were shouting slogans for the merger of Kashmir with Pakistan. It was a fighting like situation between NSF and MSF. Seeing this worst situation police and Pakistani rangers were called immediately and we all were taken into a safe hall.

Actually entire situation went out of hand because of a statement given by one of student. Our interaction with students, professor and intellectuals had just started. Suddenly a student protested this meeting blaming it a program sponsored by the ISI.

We all were also seeing impact of ISI on all our movements during this visit and here a young man had proved it.

The moment young man blamed that program was ISI sponsored, another group started shouting slogan in supports of Pakistan.

In the mean time few outsiders entered into arena and instigated to fight with opponents. JKLF supporters were shouting slogan "Elhak ke jo yaar hain, wo gadder hain, gaddar hain." (People who support merger of Azad Jammu and Kashmir with Pakistan are enemy of all Kashmiri people)

Sound of shouting slogans pro and against Pakistan were continued. We were kept safe in a separate hall. Few protesters entered in this hall also but they were kicked back soon by security personnel. We had visited there to know the opinion of Kashmiri students on Kashmir problems but become totally disappointed. We were honored with the Mementoes of University by Jammu and Kashmir university amidst chaos and were said to sit inside bus immediately. We returned our hotel in tight security.

Here I must make you clear that students who were supporting merger of Azad Jammu and Kashmir in Pakistan were habitants of Muzaffarabad and students who were supporting freedom of Kashmir from Pakistan and India both, were migrated from valley. Because of presence of police and rangers, a boiling situation that would turn into a violent scene was stopped.

Here it is important to know the formula of General Perwej Musharraf .

Probably, out of fear of international boycott because of 9/11 incidence, General Perwej Musharraf in hurry proposed a formula to divide Kashmir into seven parts, to achieve permanent and final solution of the Kashmir problem. The so called proposal of Musharraf(India did not take even notice) is full of contradictions. An acceptable view is that India has three province in its Kashmir territory. They are Jammu, Ladakh and the valley. But Musharraf again divided it on the basis of religion, ethnic and geographical calculations, into seven parts as follows;

Ladakh, the Islamic part between Himalyas and the Indus.

Kargil / Dras(Muslims).

Poonch(Muslim Contagious with Azad Kashmir)

Jammu(Muslim majority districts)

Valley

Azad Jammu and Kashmir

The Northern Region

We all know that above five parts are under Indian rule and last two are under Pakistan rule.

It was my pleasure that before the worsening the situation, I got an opportunity to interact with few students and professors. They were in favour of opening of Srinagar-Muzaffarabad Bus service and simultaneously they also said that unless and until Kashmir problem would be resolved, these bus services would not work.

■■■

Chapter 33

Perception of a Pakistani Author

The Vice Chancellor of Azad Jammu and Kashmir University had honoured with Mementoes to all the Indian journalists who had arrived . We were also presented a book by one of department of Azad Jammu and Kashmir University, "Institute of Kashmir Studies". The title of the book was "Kashmir dispute at a glance" and the author of this book was non-other than the Vice Chancellor himself Professor khan Jaman Mirza. I found this book full of misleading facts. This book was dedicated to freedom of Kashmir and was published in 1993.

Prof. Khan had pointed only those points in this book which were favouring merger of Azad Jammu and Kashmir with Pakistan. This book had been written with biased intensions. We felt total lack of neutral approach of the author. This book had been written to please the top political leaders, army personnel and the ISI of Pakistan. In the beginning, author had written: " once upon a time Azad Jammu and Kashmir was famous for its immense natural beauty but now was bleeding and burning. Kashmir was turned into hell because of cruel and inhuman policy of Indian army and Indian border security forces. Conspiracy, fraud, cheating, false promise and Oath taken in the name of religion by India had remained some of reasons behind all sorts of violence and restlessness in Azad

Jammu and Kashmir. Government of Pakistan was forced to go in United Nations organizations to report atrocities of India. India had been violating all human rights in India's Kashmir and was the sole reason behind all the problems in Kashmir. India had been suppressing the freedom movement of Kashmiri people and also had been doing propaganda in entire world that the separatist and terrorist were behind the restlessness and violence in Kashmir. India had been misleading world communities on Kashmir issue. Pakistan got success in unfolding the real face of India in United Nations organization after 1990. World communities became more aware regarding Kashmir issues".

Here we must not forget that this book is a one sided fake documentation. It was the Sardar Abdul Kayyum Khan who fought against Dogra ruler. We also must not forget that if you are an employee in any department of the Azad Jammu and Kashmir Government or in politics or doing business under the supervision of Government, then support of Government of Azad Jammu and Kashmir becomes essential for you and you have to prove yourself a staunch supporter of Government of Azad Jammu and Kashmir which has been ruled by Pakistan.

Author had dedicated all his research work complied in this book, to the people of the World and all the Nations of the world.

Nearly 46 years ago, people of Kashmir had cleared his opinion in UNO that it would be their preference to merge either in Pakistan or in India and this process would be completed under supervision of UNO in a very democratic way. People of Jammu and Kashmir were given guarantee to choose their preference according to their wish and will.

India and Pakistan both had given their consent on

above proposal proposed by Security Council of United Nations Organization. But still today this agreement had not been formulated and people of Kashmir were not allowed to show their preferences regarding merger.

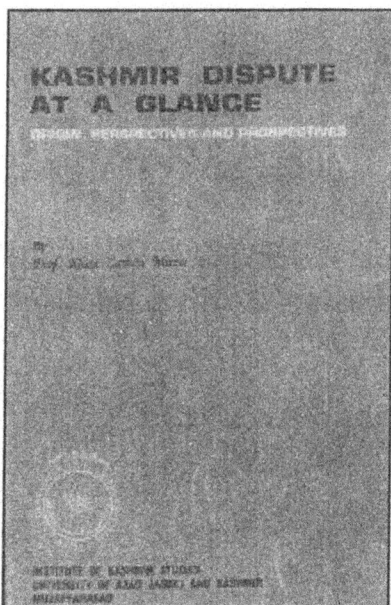

A Book written by a Pakistani author Professor Jaman Mirza

Jammu and Kashmir is a separate place in the map of United Nations. It is neither shown as a part of India or Pakistan. This is a separate state according to international law and constitution of Azad Jammu and Kashmir .

The Muslims of Jammu and Kashmir are now tired to solve the Kashmir issue with peaceful means. They have struggling since 40 years. Muslim constitutes 80 percent population of Jammu and Kashmir and now have started revolting against political dominance of India in India's Kashmir and army atrocities in Azad Jammu and Kashmir. People of Jammu and Kashmir have been sacrificing their lives for the sake of freedom and India has been openly violating human rights laws. On international forum that Kashmir is an inseparable part of India remained a permanent propaganda of India.

Author has also written that: India's first Prime minister Pandit Nehru ,during his speech inside parliament and outside in public meetings, openly accepted that Kashmir is not an integral part of India; and it is the only truth.

You must not laugh at this logic of this learned author.

According to this author the Kashmir issue is also an unsolved problem under the freedom act of India. This freedom act says that two sovereign nations will be established. One nation (Pakistan) will be born on 14th august and second nation (India) will get freedom on 15th August 1947. The Author also attracts attention on the conspiracy of Congress and Mountbatten to create the problem of Kashmir since 1947 and this problem has been stuck in the files of Security Council of UNO. India and Pakistan both are appellants there.

This book " **Kashmir dispute at a glance"** also details the history of Kashmir with its geographical status. I have already given description of history of Kashmir in previous chapters but here I want to say that Author of this book was totally biased. He writes : "On 23 march 1940, All India Muslim League passed a resolution regarding formation of a new Nation on the basis of religion, and all the Muslims of Kashmir dedicated themselves in the freedom movement".

Author also has presented some selected quotes on Kashmir written by various authors, to show the inclination of Jammu and Kashmir to merge with Pakistan.

Author Profesor Khan Jaman Mirza has put serious allegation on British viceroy and first Government General of India Lord Mountbatten telling him a conspirator on the issue of Kashmir.

At the end of the book author appeals to the international community. He writes : "Muslim of India's part of Kashmir must come forward to convince international communities that this part of Kashmir is not a controversial one, but it is the issue of their self respect, self decision and right to show their preferences. We appeal to the international community to support in the fight of freedom movement and protect their human rights. Here we must clear that India and Pakistan both have infringed the right of self preference to the people of Kashmir and thus both the Nations have broken their promise resulting a big tyranny on Kashmir people. Please interfere to stop it".

I find author is biased and book is full of biased logic. Most of the description are controversial and most of the facts are fake. This book is a kind of propaganda where only one part of Kashmir issue is being projected.

Sardar Abdul Kayyum Khan has written forword of this book.

Sardar A.K.Khan is known as Mujahid e Awwal, remained president continuously for four terms and the then was a Prime Minister of Azad Jammu and Kashmir. So Mr. Prime Minister of Azad Jammu and Kashmir had written the forword of this book making it clear that this is one sided.

Sardar A.K.Khan has remained pioneer in operating armed struggler in Jammu and Kashmir since 1947; was chairman of National Kashmir Committee, toured around the globe, attained hundreds of seminars and discussion on Kashmir issue. He is also an author of many political and religious books and always have remained in focus. He also served two terms as leader of opposition in assembly of Azad Jammu and Kashmir. He is the man who first formed Azad Kashmir Battalion and this Battalion still serves in Azad Jammu and Kashmir as 19th Battalion. After Azad Kashmir Battalion, he formed "operation one brigade" Battalion that in the course of time became famous in history as "Kayyum Brigade". This kayyum brigade was responsible for killing of hundreds of people at Udi and punch region from 1947 to 1949.

After the agreement of seize fire at UNO in 1949. Kayyum Brigade was dissolved and Sardar A.K.Khan entered in Kashmir politics under the banner of Jammu and Kashmir Muslim Conference.

This man Sardar A.K. Khan, pioneer of armed struggle, now has become tired of armed struggle.

Now, he accepts that Kashmir problem can be solved through peaceful dialogues only.

I personally came on conclusion after interacting with Sardar A.K. Khan that armed struggle for freedom have slipped from their hand and reached into the hands of various terrorist organizations.

Now they have started seeing solution in peaceful means.

Here a question raises for everybody. Leaders like Sardar A.K. Khan and Amanullah Khan, who have changed their mind set and started advocating Non-violence means of protest and project Kashmir as secular region, can ever will win the confidence of migrated Kashmiri Pundits, who were forced to migrate on gun point.

They demand freedom on the basis of Muslim majority. Can they give guarantee for the safety of minorities (Hindu, Sikh, Baudhs & others).

■■■

Chapter 34
Innocent Beggars

In Muzaffarabad, I saw such a real face of freedom struggle of Kashmir, that never imagined earlier. It was really painful to see leaders doing inhuman politics in the name of freedom of Kashmir. Since Indo-Pak partition, leaders who have been supporting merger of Jammu and Kashmir with Pakistan, or Separatist leaders harping for the separate state of Kashmir or Militant organizations shouting slogans for the complete freedom of undivided Kashmir, all have been giving false hope to Kashmiri people. I realized this painful fact during visit of Muzaffarabad. Many people have crossed line of control hoping to get real freedom but have been living a life of hell. No one had imagined while crossing line of control that they would face such worst condition. They were living a life worst than slave. We got an opportunity to visit some refugee camps. Our all the movements were fixed by the ISI and it was very much clear that we would not get even a glimpse of hard realities. Only sponsored people would be allowed to meet us. I was looking for an opportunity to meet with a genuine refugee to know the real condition of refugee camps. Though it was difficult because of strong vigil of the ISI people. I came out from Sangam Hotel and walked up to nearby Gilani Chauk. There I was shocked to see many innocent children beggars.

Who were those innocent beggars ? All those little girls and little boys begging as it were their only way of living. I called one of little girl and asked about her identity. She told that she was the daughter of a Mujahir (refugee) who came here from India's part of Kashmir by crossing line of control. She was little grown up girl and looked like in the age of11 or 12 years. She was also sensible. She along with her family were living in a Mujahir Camp (refugee camp) opened in one of school of Muzaffarabad. They had no work accept begging. Each and every children beggars were sons and daughter of Mujahirs   (refugee came from India's kashmir). All the Muhajirs were hammered from both the sides. They neither got freedom nor any work to fill the stomach of their kids and other members of their families.

It was a crying moment for me and I wanted to meet with the families of these innocent beggars. I was talking with innocent beggars and was not present in hotel, could be a problem in the eye of the ISI people. I returned back to hotel thinking to visit one of refugee camp according to earlier plan. I saw the most painful face of propaganda of freedom struggle of Kashmir generated by politicians, separatist leaders and militant organizations. I shared this fact with some of hotel staffs they told me that under the influence of some separatist leaders, people had crossed the line of control and had facing most cruel life in refugee camps. Whoever enters in Azad Jammu and Kashmir from India's Kashmir was given status of Mujahir (refugee). After that they forced to live a life of slave. Because of fear of the ISI some of the Mujahirs have become mentally sick. Some of Mujahirs were put into jail because the ISI people did not like them and treated them as spy. I came across the most cruel facts of innocent Mujahirs. Their children never knew about books and pen; they do begging to fill their stomach and indicated towards the darkest future.

■■■

Chapter 35
Refugee Camp: A Hell on Earth

Finally we media people were told to visit one of refugee camp. Relief commissioner of Azad Jammu and Kashmir briefed us that approximate 35,000 people from India's part of Kashmir had migrated in Azad Jammu and Kashmir in previous one and half decades, and migration was still continued. Maximum number of migrated people had reached Muzaffarabad. Government of Azad Jammu and Kashmir had created refugee camps specially for migrants from India's Kashmir.

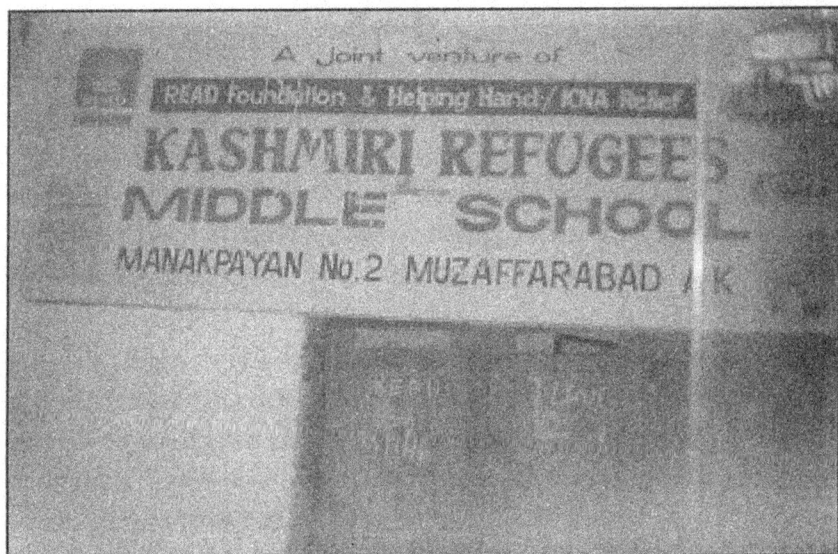

A refugee camp, running in a Government school at Muzaffarabad

Apart from nine refugee camps in Muzaffarabad, two in Mirpur and four in district Bagh are also being managed by Azad Jammu and Kashmir. In the records of Government of Azad Jammu and Kashmir, every Mujahir gets rupees 700 per month. 700 Pakistani rupees are equal to 600 Indian rupees. You can imagine how a person can live thirty days in seven hundred only. Though on paper Azad Jammu and Kashmir has separate identity but it runs on Pakistan's currency.

Here, I understood the reasons behind begging the innocent children of Mujahirs. After the briefing by relief commissioner Mohammed Altalib, we were taken to one of refugee camps in Muzaffarabad . It was a temporary structure, made in a school. There was total lack of basic amenities. Though it was clearly visible that the ISI had tried to made this refugee camp, a better place for living but reality was wide open. Few refugee were allowed to interact with as (I knew they were ISI sponsored). One of refugee Jhagar Khan told as that he crossed line of control because of atrocities of Indian border security force. Another refugee who was sub-inspector in India's Jammu-Kashmir, told us that Indian Border Security Force had doubt on him that he was working for a terrorist organization. He was arrested and tortured without any reason. The moral of the story that they revealed to us that it was the atrocities of Indian army that forced them to migrate from India's part of Kashmir to Azad Jammu and Kashmir.

I was searching a genuine Mujahir who could give us real picture of refugee camps. I saw a Mujahir watching us silently. I went to him and asked his name. He was Adbul Sattar. I said him to meet me at Hotel Sangam. Though it was a risk but I had taken. It was also not an easy task for Abdul Sattar to come and meet me at hotel Sangam. I was

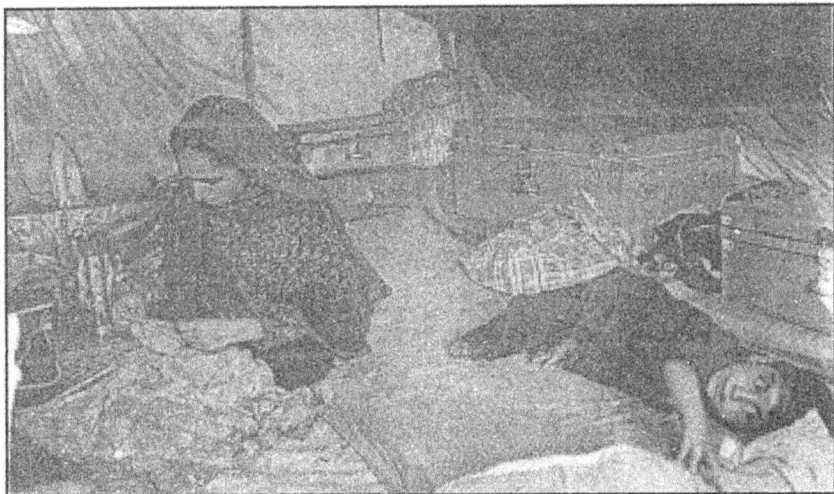

A Kashmiri Mujahir family, migrated to Muzaffarabad

confident from inside that Abdul Sattar would take risk and surely would come to meet me. We returned back to hotel but remained outside the gate of hotel. I was waiting for Abdul Sattar. I had taken a great risk. Abdul Sattar could be arrested by the ISI for the meeting with me without their permission. It was not a long wait. I saw Abdul Sattar along with his friend (another refugee) coming towards the gate of hotel. He was stopped by few person. I understood the presence of the ISI people. I lost my cool and run towards the gate of hotel. After some heated discussion, I could able to take them inside hotel.

Abdul Sattar and his friend had migrated here from Baramulla (India's Kashmir) in search of freedom but became slaves. He had been crying over his decision to migrate from his homeland. Abdul Sattar straight forward said that all Mujahirs (migrated people) living in various refugee camps were in very bad conditions. Mujahirs blamed their own decision to migrate from their homes under a fake dream. The Mujahirs live here under the fear of the ISI. Only those Mujahirs who became agents of the

ISI, were living a better life. Some Mujahirs joined the freedom movement (in Jehad) to sustain their lives. Rest of the Mujahirs were living like slaves. Abdul Sattar personally knew 5000 refugees who wanted to go back to their homes (india's Kashmir) but now they were helpless. If they would cross line of control, Indian Border Security Force would arrest them. Abdul sattar and his friend were requesting me to take their appeal to the leaders of India. They wanted to go back their homes and only Government of India could make this possible. They were really sorry for their act of migration and apologies for that. They wanted to return in mass if Indian government forgives them for their misdeed. The moral of the story was that all the Mujahirs were in very painful situation and their children were forced for begging to fill their stomach. All the mujahirs were also very angry with local Hurriyat leaders. Leaders like Ghulam Nabi Naushebi, Ghulam Ahmed Saufi, Yusuf Naim, Afhaf kadari, Ashraf Saroj etc. had been selling Mujahirs and became rich. The ISI agents and locals do insult females of Mujahirs family, said friend of Abdul Sattar(Few were forcefully pushed in skin trade). When they oppose, they were threatened to put into jail. The most common allegation that the ISI put on Mujahirs was an allegation of spying.

I was satisfied with the conversation with Abdul sattar and his friend and now was thinking how they would go back to their refugee camp. The ISI people might catch them. Abdul Sattar and his friend went out from my hotel's room. I tried to know about their welfare but could not get any information. I felt helpless.

Later I met with some more Mujahirs. They questioned on the name of Azad Jammu and Kashmir. They had experienced that name Azad was a greatest fraud. You could find hundreds of Abdul Sattar who could give you real picture of Azad Jammu and Kashmir and Mujahirs. But you also can get some people who speak infavour of freedom but at the point of gun. Here I must quote a statement of Jahur Ahmed Batt. Jahur Ahmed Batt was the younger brother of Maqbul Bhatt, who was hanged in India. Jahur Ahmed said: " people living in India's part of Kashmir enjoy greater freedom".

All most all the Mujahirs also accept this fact. But they are helpless now. Jahur Ahmed Batt are one of important leader of JKLF and son of Maqbul Bhatt, Shaukat Bhatt are also a strong leader of JKLF. Citizens of Azad Jammu and Kashmir also say that their freedom struggle has been hijacked by outside terrorists and all of them are being nourished by the ISI.

We also met with such people, who were part of terrorist activities but when they came to know the reality of freedom struggle, they changed their way. Few people also said that they were alive because of guns and they would die with the guns. We met with former commander of Tahreek-ul-mujahhidin, Mukhtaar Mohamood. He looked depressed.

Few Mujahirs narrated their last wish to us. They wanted to return back homes. They wanted to return back to India. They told us to worship the land of India; that way , it might fetch them some peace of mind.

■■■

Chapter 36

Searching for Roots and Identity

It is in history that since 1947, when Pakistan was born with Indo-Pakistani partition, to 1960, people of Azad Jammu and Kashmir had not been given right to vote. In all these years election did not happen in Azad Jammu and Kashmir.

From 1960 to 1975 General Ayub Khan was in power in Pakistan and Sikander Mirza remained president of Azad Jammu and Kashmir. No any political movement was allowed in Azad Jammu and Kashmir. General Ayub khan had accepted to go for public consensus and showed his liberalism to achieve democratic system of administration. Thus in 1960, a fundamental democratic act came in existence in Azad Jammu and Kashmir and first time people participated in the presidential election. This election was followed by election of Pakistan Occupied Kashmir Parishad.

Every citizen along with all the Mujahirs understand that Azad Jammu and Kashmir is being ruled by Ministry of Kashmir Affairs running under Government of Pakistan. All the administrative works is being supervised by an official of joint secretary level, known as chief advisor in Azad Jammu and Kashmir.

All the important posts of Kashmir Parishad of Azad Jammu and Kashmir was filled with Pakistani officers. Only

A unfortunate Kashmiri Child at Muzaffarabad

a Pakistani could be appointed for the post of Inspector General of Police and finance secretary. Officially called accountant general of Azad Jammu and Kashmir.

It is important to know that according to 1974 constitution of Pakistan, prepared during the regime of Bhutto, all the powers to handle administrative works of Azad Jammu and Kashmir was vested in Kashmir Parishad. Prime Minister of Pakistan was an autonomous chairman of Kashmir Parishad and were responsible to look after the work of Kashmir Parishsd with 6 nominated members.

All the ruler of Pakistan, from General Ayub Khan to Prime-Minister Bhutto or General Ziya-ul-Haque, ruled Azad Jammu and Kashmir according to their wish and will. They had implemented Marshall law and appointed their men on the top posts, ban political activities and did whatever they wanted to rule on Pakistan occupied Jammu and Kashmir. Though they have been calling it Azad Jammu and Kashmir.

Even the Prime-minister and president of Azad Jammu and Kashmir remained a toy in the hands of ruler of Pakistan.

See the irony of Azad Jammu and Kashmir. Neither it is a part of Pakistan nor a separate state. Even the prime minister of Azad Jammu and Kashmir holds a very limited right. It never makes any difference that Pakistan is being governed by army or by a democratic government, people of Azad Jammu and Kashmir are bound to live under their influence and rule.

It is a hard fact that fate of Azad Jammu and Kashmir is totally depend on the act and actions of Islamabad and people of Azad Jammu and Kashmir are destined to face atrocities of Pakistan administration. They are helpless and still search their roots and identity.

■■■

Chapter 37

They Live with a Dream: Kashmir Will Become Pakistan

During our visit at Mirpur- Kotli region of Muzaffarabad, we clearly experienced an ongoing freedom movement in entire region. The people of this region wanted freedom but it was almost impossible to achieve it. The Prime Minister of Azad Jammu and Kashmir Sardar Sikander Hyat Khan had given an statement to us: "If people of Azad Jammu and Kashmir will vote against Pakistan, I will leave this place and will go to settle in Pakistan". With

the same approach other political leaders, ministers, top bureaucrats, all have announced that Jammu and Kashmir will merge with Pakistan". Now, a question arises ! Why a violent armed struggle for freedom is being operated in India's Jammu and Kashmir?

In the last moment of our Pakistan's journey, we were invited by Major General

Sadre Riyasat of Azad Jammu and Kashmir General Mohammed Anwar Khan

Anwar Khan of Azad Jammu and Kashmir. It was a programme of dinner and discussion together. Though we had been enjoying and attending various lunch and dinner programs organized by top leaders of Pakistan Occupied Kashmir and Pakistan, I was giving this invitation some more importance. I was expecting some strange happening that had not happened with us during the entire Pakistan journey.

We reached the venue of dinner and discussion program but got shock to see crowd. Only Army Personnel, Police Officers the ISI People were there to welcome us . We found very few journalists and other guests. Why Azad Jammu and Kashmir is called Pakistan occupied Kashmir, was clearly visible there. Presence of army, police and the ISI had made us tense. We were expecting a lighter discussion and tasty food but here, the scenario was totally different. I was hearing crying sound of silence. No body was ready to interact with anybody. At last, we got the smell of tasty food. We were served a variety of tasty foods.

I found some written words on every plate. It was either in Urdu or Farsi language. I took help from one of my Urdu knowing journalist friend. I thought my friend would tell me that it was a message of religious epic Koran. My friend Salim Pandit read the written massage on the Plate and started talking some other thing. I knew that Salim Pandit had very good command over Urdu and Farsi both. Then, why he was trying to avoid me ? I put pressure on him but he remained adamant not to reveal those written words. At last, I got angry and told him that it was the last moment of our friendship. My last sentence worked. Salim Pandit made it clear to me about the written words on every plate and other pots. The written words were "Kashmir will be Pakistan". Now I got relaxed. I knew that the mystery of message written on every plate. I knew the conspiracy of each and every political leader, the army, police and the ISI. They all had one goal. They all wanted to see Kashmir merged with Pakistan. They all were playing with the emotions of all the Kashmiri people living on either side of the line of control.

To show the world at large, there is a democracy in Azad Jammu and Kashmir, but only those citizens are allowed to cast their vote, who either sign or give thumb stamp on the paper of acceptance that they vote for the merger of Kashmir with Pakistan.

Now you can understand the mind set of rulers of Pakistan and Pakistan occupied Kashmir. They want to continue armed struggle for freedom in India's Jammu and Kashmir and dream Azad Jammu and Kashmir to be merged with Pakistan.

It seems that if not today then certainly tomorrow, new generation will accept that Azad Jammu and Kashmir is a part of Pakistan.

Our friends enjoyed tasty food and I enjoyed my thought and Pakistan's reality with the empty plate in hand. My eyes were focused on written massage that I could not read but understood now. This slogan was the extreme of Pakistani propaganda that even people of Azad Jammu and Kashmir wanted to merge with Pakistan.

Here, I must inform you that according to election rules of 1970 of Azad Jammu and Kashmir only those candidates can fight election who support the merger of Azad Jammu and Kashmir with Pakistan. And whoever will oppose the merger of Azad Jammu and Kashmir with Pakistan will be deemed a conspirator against Pakistan, Pakistani army, the ISI and Azad Jammu and Kashmir.

In the election of 1996 and 2006, candidates, who did not sign on declaration paper that clearly stated about acceptance of merger of Azad Jammu and Kashmir with Pakistan, were declared invalid to fight election. According to Constitutional act 1974 Part 7(2) of Azad Jammu and Kashmir, whoever will show his/her non-acceptance regarding the merger of Kashmir with the Pakistan, will not be allowed in any democratic process. Now, see the next step. After wining election and before sitting on the chair of Prime-Minister, President, Speaker or any minister, they take oath that they will work in favour and in the interests of Pakistan and will support merger of Kashmir with Pakistan.

On the one hand political leaders take this kind of oath and on the other hand, citizens of Azad Jammu and Kashmir are treated like foreigners in Pakistan.

People of Azad Jammu and Kashmir don't have any right to vote in Pakistan. They even don't have any right to file cases in the Supreme Court of Pakistan. They can't open their offices in Pakistan and don't have any right to share in the budget of Government of Pakistan. The Government of Azad Jammu and Kashmir runs on the wish and will of Government of Pakistan.

According to section 56 of constitution of the Azad Jammu and Kashmir, all the administration rights are vested in the hands of Government of Pakistan.

Look at this example:

During Presidential regime of General Ayub Khan in Pakistan a Inspector General of Police had taken resignation from Late K.H.Khurshid, the then President of Azad Jammu and Kashmir, and had put him into jail. You will be surprised to know that H.K.Khurshid once were personal secretary of Mohammed Ali Jinnah. During ZulfikarAli Bhutto's regime, elected president of Azad Jammu and Kashmir were forced to step down from his post by Deputy Inspector General. During the regime of

President General Zia-Ul-Haque, a Brigadier Hyat Khan were given control of Azad Jammu and Kashmir and he ruled continuously for seven years.

The Minister of Kashmir Affairs of Pakistan Janab Abbasi once said in a press conference that he could send a constable from Pakistan to join as president of Azad Jammu and Kashmir.

History is the witness of all the unfair and biased elections of Azad Jammu and Kashmir. Government of Pakistan declares result according to its wish and will. Pakistan has made Azad Jammu and Kashmir totally dependent on it.

It was the last moment of our visit at Muzaffarabad. Our next destination was Gilgit. Actually to visit Gilgit was not mentioned in our passport's visa. SAFMA's General secretary and senior journalist Imtiyaz Alam , representative of team of Indian journalists Vinod Kumar Sharma and SAFMA General Secretary of Pakistan's chapter Mustasar Javed all took initiatives, they directly met with President General Parwej Musharraf and took permission to visit Gilgit. So we all felt grateful to them. Earlier no any Indian was allowed to visit Gilgit. It was a big and brave heart of General Parwej Musharraf that we Indian Journalists got an opportunity to visit Gilgit.

■ ■ ■

Chapter 38
Gilgit: The Northern Region

The last and most important destination of our visit was Gilgit. It was impossible for an indian to reach Gilgit. I had a lot of assumption and presumptions about the Northern region . Gilgit was part of undivided Kashmir and presently it was under the rule of pakistan. Government of Pakistan with a planned thought, had not given constitutional status to Gilgit.

The reasons is clear enough. Pakistan don't want to project Northern region as a part of undivided Kashmir. They want to keep it away from the Kashmir controversy. Pakistan is looking for an opportunity to make it an integral part of Pakistan and till then want to rule on this region without any controversy. Due to these reasons, Pakistan never issues visa to any Indian to visit this place.

Though we also had not been given visa to visit Gilgit but it was the greatness of General Parwej Musharraf that we got permission to visit this place.

Gilgit is bordered with NWFP of Afghanistan and Pakistan and close to   Chhin jiyang of China.

We were given schedule of Gilgit visit. We had to fly from Rawalpindi Airport. Early in the morning we moved from Muzaffarabad to reach Islamabad. We reached Rawalpindi at time. As we said many times in previous

Gilgit, once was a part of undivided Kashmir

memories that the ISI has kept close visit all the time on us. Wherever we reached, found members of JKLF waiting for us. There was no plan to stay at Rawalpindi but leaders of JKLF like Altaf Ahmed Kadri, Salim Farukh, Rafique etc.

wanted to meet with Indian journalist. Those separatist leaders were known as think tank of JKLF. We met them. All the leaders were appreciating Indian Prime Minister Manmohan Singh and President of Pakistan General Parwej Mushrraf for initiating process of peaceful dialogues . JKLF leaders were also in favour of interactions between intellectuals and artists of both the Nations.

They said: "The peace process between both the nations had been started, so there was no need of any armed freedom struggle in India`s Kashmir. But both the nations must promise to give a sense of satisfaction to them (freedom fighters) that something was happening concrete to solve the Kashmir problem. JKLF leaders also show their support for Muzaffarabad Sri Nagar Bus service. They also said that representatives of Jammu, Kashmir and also Laddakh must be called to participate in every peace dialogues. If people of Jammu and Laddakh want to go with India, they don't have objection.

I asked a question to them regarding reaction of Supremo of Hijbul Mujahhidin and Chairman of Muttehada Council, Syed Salauddin. They answered that they had nothing to do with Syed Salauddin. The JKLF leaders were in favour of opening a gate of trust that could allow all Kashmiris to meet their family members living in either part of line of control.

The JKLF leaders also said that there must not be one sided visit of security agencies on Srinagar-Muzaffarabad bus-service. There must be a joint security system and joint control. They were fearing misdeeds of the ISI.

■ ■ ■

Chapter 39
Baltistan National Movement

After the meeting with JKLF leaders, we were taken to Rawalpindi airport and were shifted in a small aero plane F-37. Thus the F-37 took us into sky and showed us the great picture of nature. Air hostess informed us that we could see snow covered hills, famous with the name of Nanga Parwat. It was the same region, where an Indian Air force plane had crashed with the thick layer of snow and was sank into it during 1971 Indo-Pakistani war. No body got trace of that Indian fighter plane. Air-hostess had some great feeling when she was informing us about the crash of Indian fighter plane. Whatever it was wonderful sight. It was almost a one hour fly. F-37 landed on the track of Gilgit airport. Hundreds of JKLF supporters, with banners and posters in hands, were shouting slogans. We saw this scene from the window of the plane. JKLF supporters were informed about arrival of Indian media and they had shown their existence in no time.

We were taken in a hotel of Department of Tourism by a mini tourist bus. According to schedule we had to meet with the leaders of local organizations. The day had almost passed. It was almost evening with less than zero degree Celsius temperature. We could see snow covered land. It was an unforgettable sight. It was an unforgettable moment. Beauty lies in the nature. I can not narrate my feeling in words. We were served tea and breakfast by hotel staffs. I thank God and appreciated zeal of General Parwej Mushrraf who allowed us to visit Gilgit.

Chinar Bagh of Gilgit

First December 2004 became an unforgettable day for me. Earlier, Gilgit was a great destination for international tourists but terrorism had affected tourism industry in a big way. Separatist leaders had cropped up there. Constitutionally, Gilgit is not part of Pakistan but it is being ruled by Pakistan. This phenomenon created a sense of dissatisfaction in the hearts and minds of people of this region.

A CEO (chief executive officer) handles all the administrative works of this northern region of Pakistan. Minister of Kashmir affairs also holds the post of CEO. CEO rules on this region through appointed secretary and Deputy secretary of this region.

We were informed that Faizal Saleh Hyat was the then Minister of Kashmir affairs and CEO of Northern region.

　　　　　　An Encounter with Pakistan's Reality

Secretary and deputy secretary were also from Pakistan. National political parties of Pakistan had been fighting election in Northern region. These political parties were Pakistan people's party and Pakistani Muslim league.

Baltistan is bordered with China and nature has poured its immense beauty on it. 90 percent area of this region is covered with chain of hills. Whoever came to meet us, advocated separate Northern region. Terrorism has been replaced with separatism. Local citizens of Baltistan now openly discuss about their freedom from Pakistan's rule. Now they show their dissatisfaction and protest against administration of Pakistan. What we saw in Mirpur-Kotli region to Muzaffarabad, was clearly visible here. Workers of Baltistan National Movement (BNM) have been demanding Azad Baltistan Ganrajya (Republic of free Baltistan) since long time. I got an opportunity to interact with the General Secretary of BNM, Shujat Ali Khan. He was totally against rule of Pakistan and was demanding a separate state making Laddakh and Baltistan into one. Local chief of JKLF (Amanullah's group), Zia-Ul-Hque, also said that he wanted to see Gilgit and Baltistan, a separate free state. Pakistan had occupied this region forcefully and voice of common citizens was being suppressed.

He also admitted that armed struggle in India's part of Kashmir had been operated with the direct support of Pakistan.

We came on conclusion that freedom movement was on rise in Gilgit Baltistan region as it was in Pakistan Occupied Kashmir.

River Sindhu floats across Gilgit region. Once upon time it was a great tourist region and tourists around the globe used to visit this place even after facing lots of hardship. Whoever comes here, feels proud and that is the magic of this region. Empty hotels and restaurants still look for those great global tourists, once they used to fill their places. A blow on tourism industry have made many unemployed. Terrorism entered in this region with the destruction of USSR (Russia), said one of hotelier.

After the 9/11 incidence tourist from America and Europe have stopped visiting in this region.

You can see costliest cars like Pazero, Cruse, Toyota, Pardo..on the roads of Gilgit and Baltistan but now without tourist. As this region is bordered with China and Government of Pakistan did not put extra tax of any foreign goods, China's goods are flooded in this region. You can see a special China market in Gilgit. An another China medicine market is also running but all in bad condition. Terrorism has stolen the smile of this region. We got information that the ISI tortures not only common people of this region but they also don't spare journalists. They already had cancelled registration of an important local weekly news paper.

We were served tasty food in dinner. When I entered in our hotel's room, saw a thin blanket on the bed and a kerosene oil heater. I was thinking about minus 0' temperature and a thin blanket but it worked greatly. Heat of kerosene oil heater and thin blanket made that night quite comfortable and I had really a sound sleep.

Next morning we had to return back to Rawalpindi. Visti to Gilgit was like a dream came true.

■■■

Chapter 40
Reality of Northern Region

It is essential to know the facts about Northern region or the Gilgit. Gilgit is being projected as hill capital region of Pakistan. International tourists have been visiting this region with the prior permission of Pakistan, but reality is altogether different. The constitutional status of this northern region has not been cleared till now.

Pakistan always has been showing its double face on this northern region. Political leaders along with Pakistan army and the ISI have been looking for an opportunity to declare this northern region as a permanent part of Pakistan. Pakistan holds complete control over Northern region and is enough confident tomake it in favour of him, if such situation arises. Pakistan don't want to show Northern region as

Book written on the judgement on the writ petition filed by the frmer Justice Abdul Majeed Malik

Pakistan occupied region. It is a matter of surprise that once undivided land of Kashmir; captured by Pakistan has been declared as separate land. 5703 square kilometers of land comes under Azad Jammu and Kashmir, generally known as Pakistan occupied Kashmir and 72, 495 square kilometers of land is known as Northern Region, it was already captured and ruled by Pakistan. People of this province directly blame Pakistan for making them slaves under a well thought conspiracy. They also blame on Pakistan for making an illegal boundary agreement with China and delivering them 5180 square kilometers land. This piece of land is situated in the north of Mintaka. A local resident, Kazi Barkat told us that they usually saw activities of Chinese army on this land. Now, I could realize that why Pakistan, under an agreement had delivered this piece of land to China. An interesting fact I realized there, like the people of Azad Jammu and Kashmir, people of northern region were also demanding to get back this China occupied land. The three representatives of this region Malik Masken, Hazi Ameer Jan and Sheikh Abdul Jan had filed a petition in the High Court of Azad Jammu and Kashmir for considering Northern region a Constitutional part of Azad Jammu and Kashmir under 1974 Constitutional act. They had requested to provide all the fundamental rights to the people of Baltistan and Gilgit taking them as a part of Azad Jammu and Kashmir.

A decision of Chief Justice Abdul Mazeed Malik came on 8 march 1993. They had ordered administration of Azad Jammu and Kashmir to take administrative control of Northern Region and the Government of Pakistan was ordered to help Azad Jammu and Kashmir in setting the score. High Court had also ordered to provide them Constitutional system like legislative assembly, legislative council and civil service under 1974 Constitutional Act to provide basic amenities to the people of Northern Region. The Government of Pakistan had put his point of view that high court of Azad Jammu and Kashmir had not even the right to hear such litigation but High Court had rejected the plea of Pakistan and intimated them that 1974 Constitutional Act provides them all these rights. The court also accepted that entire Northern Region was part of undivided Kashmir.

Government of Pakistan filed another writ petition in Pakistan Supreme Court against the judgment of High court of Azad Jammu and Kashmir. Decision came on 28th may 1999. Supreme Court of Pakistan had ordered Government of Pakistan to constitute council of Northern Region within six months to provide fundamental rights to all people of this region. The people of northern region have all the rights to enjoy legal amenities through an elected government. On the basis of this judgment council of Northern region was formed and Gilgit became administrative headquarter of Northern region. Few people presented me a book on constitutional status of Northern region. I read the entire book and reached on following conclusion.

Just two weeks before the partition, On first August 1947, King of Kashmir, Maharaja Hari Singh had appointed Brigadier Ghausara Singh as a administrator (Governor) of Gilgit. But when Maharaja Hari Singh signed a contract to merge in India on 26th October 1947, controversies spread like fire.

NWFP tribes man of Gilgit Pathan Afridi revolted. On first november, 1947, Brigadier Ghausara Singh was arrested and kept under house arrest and the flag of Pakistan was hosted. Same way Baltistan was also captured. A seize fire was announced in UNO on first January 1948 and later karanchi agreement took place in 1949. Government of Pakistan, All Jammu and Kashmir Muslim conference had signed on this agreement.

After that, from first July 1950, Pakistan took complete control over Northern Region and since then people of this region have been struggling for freedo

■ ■ ■

Chapter 41
A Journey across Karakoram

We were aware that our stay at Gilgit was very short and in next morning we had to get ready for return journey. We had been given a tourist information guide by Tourist Department of Pakistan. For the sake of gathering knowledge I read this tourist guide. According to the description of this tourist guide, from May to September remains the best months to visit Gilgit, otherwise in rest of the months entire Gilgit region remains under zero degree temperature. It was December and we all were facing freezing cold at Gilgit. Almost just 10 kilometers away from our stay, there were a chain of hills famous for the Baudh inscription, Baudh pictures and Baudh religious massages. And just 11 kilometers away from our stay there was a monuments known as victory stand (vijay smark) and named as Taj Mahal - made 700 years ago. We could reach there in just twenty minutes by jeep but it was not in our schedule. We had to return back to Rawalpindi.

We all media people gathered in the lobby of hotel. Within few minutes we had to move to take seat inside plane but suddenly we were informed that due to bad weather, plane could not take off, so we had to stay at Gilgit till weather became good for taking off.

This information came to me as good news. We were going to stay at Gilgit for some more time. We started

Hills of highest peak at Karakoram Marg

making a plan to see some historical monuments of Gilgit but then again, we were informed that our entire plan was changed. Weather did not show any sign to become better so management had decided to continue our journey by bus. It was an exciting moment for me. Whatever the place I could not able to see, I never imagined to see, will see now. From Gilgit to Rawalpindi, it was a journey of almost 900 kilometers. We got information that we would be taken via the Karakoram road that was constructed on Pakistan-China border and was still known as Old Silk Road. From Gilgit to Rawalpindi, an exciting journey was ahead.

Karakoram is situated at the maximum height on the earth and encircled by the highest hills.

Since centuries, Tourist wanted to see this place, even at once in their life-time. A bus entered into hotel campus. We all put our hand luggage on our seat and move forward to Market. We were told that journey would start after an hour. It was a weekly holiday, so market was closed. Only a few shops were open.

Author with Journalist Vinod Kumar Sharma on Karakoram Marg

Our few friends tried to purchase world famous Chinese medicines like Shilajeet, pain reliever ointment etc. from Chinese medicine stores.

Now the journey had started. Weather might be not good for taking off for a plane but while we were inside a bus, the weather looked fabulous. The bus was heading towards Karakoram in between high hills and floating rivers. We could see from moving bus hundreds and thousands feet deep land. It was generating fear, everybody's heart were beating high but it was also a great moment of excitement. We were breathing every moment in the lap of nature. What a sight! Immemorial, wonderful, magical. The history of Karakoram is of centuries old. It was situated at such height and at such place where borders of China, India, Tajakistan (part of USSR) all meet. If you keep yourself in the centre of Karakoram, then you are at 255 kilometers away from China, India, Pakistan, Tajakistan and Afghanistan(equal distance from all these nations). You can understand the importance of Karakoram for all the

Author with rangers, photograph taken at Gilgit

nations which are situated at equal distance from Karakoram.

China & Pakistan understood the importance of karakoram and made an excellent Raj Marg (National Highway). Earlier, it was dross road to be used by businessmen who could travel on horse or cross the way just by walking. Because of this Karakoram road, China-Pakistani friendship have become stronger. Historians say that from 100 years before Christ to 900 years after Christ, this road were known as Old Silk Road. Businessmen from the region of Mediterranean Sea were doing business with Asian businessmen using this Old Silk Road. This road was also witness of journey of Baudh religion from India to Tibet and then China through its disciples and followers. Ancient Baudh Bhikshu used to travel using this Old Silk Road. Historians also say that prophet of Islam Paigamber Mohammed had come through this way between 570 to 632 after Christ.

Chinese philosopher Huen Sang, a follower of Baudh religion, had discovered India by travelling via Gilgit and Swat valley.

Changez Khan had come through this Old Silk Road and captured Peshwar and Lahore in 1220. In between 1271 to 1275, famous traveler, Marco Polo had travelled through this road to complete his journey from Venice to China. Moghuls had captured from middle Asia to Delhi by utilizing this route in 1398. From 1526 to 1739 Mughals ruled India and from Delhi to this region (Gilgit). In 1586 Mugle Azam Akbar had conquered Kashmir and travelled through this Silk Road. In 1612 British India had entered India through this road for business and set up the foundation of British rule.

In 1932 German mountaineers tried to touch the peak of Nanga Parvat at Karakoram but they failed. Again they tried in 1934 and reached up to the height of 7705 meters. In this mountaineering expedition four German mountaineers and six luggage carriers lost their lives. Still today this region is the first choice for mountaineers and considered a place to be touched by only brave. We reached Karakoram. I was really excited. This was the place which bind China and Pakistan in a business and diplomatic relationship, and this was the place which was also very important in war like situation. Though Pakistan had been telling on international forum that they never had any interference in this region but we were seeing one after another army posts during all the way, where Pakistan Army and rangers were deputed on duty. At Karakoram, we knew a fact that you could purchase any Chinese goods without paying any tax. There were many restaurant and dhabas on the long road of Karakoram. Most of them were serving only Chinese foods. Here you could buy anything that was made by china. From hand made painting to electronic items to luxury cars, everything was available there without tax. We stayed there for very short time. Dark Hills of Karakoram were creating fear. This was also landslide prone area. Actually during making of roads dynamites were greatly used to break the rocks and that created big holes in-between two rocks. Today separated big stones are prone to fall.

Whatever we were at Karakoram and it was a biggest achievement for all of us. Being a journalist or being just a tourist, to see Karakoram always remained a treat.

We were told that our bus would pass through Baltistan and Swat valley. These areas were notorious for terrorists and fundamentalists. Here Pakistan army also remains helpless.

It was a very difficult journey but exciting. Here I want to give few information. This road is really very important in war like situation. This road had been constructed after 1962 Indo-China war. China has constructed this road just because to develop deep friendship with Pakistan and hold his influence in this region. In 1965 China has constructed this road for the smooth communication up to the border of both the nations Pakistan and China. It was a two lane road and had been constructed keeping in mind that even a heavy Army truck loaded with arms and ammunition could run on this road easily.

It was so difficult region that it took fifteen years in completing the construction of roads. It was obvious that China and Pakistan both had delivered their best in making this road, in terms of technical assistance from Pakistan and monetary assistance from China.

Now this old Silk road has been converted into 805 long kilometers national highway. This Karakoram road starts at the distance of hundred kilometers from the capital Islamabad. This place is called Ebtabad Haveliyan. This

National Highway starts from Ebtabad and crosses Manshera, Takot, Besham, Patan, Chillas, Gilgit, Hunja and reached at the border of China. It touches height of 1600 feet at China border. Probably it is alone road that has been constructed at this height. Baudh architecture and other symbols of Budh religion attracts attention during journey through this roads. As I already had narrated that Karakoram passage of this Rajya Marg (Highway) was land slide prone area and God had saved us from two land slides. It was a big snow ball that suddenly fall with big sound in front of our bus and second time we just had passed and heard the bang of falling stone. It had created furor inside everybody's heart. We just had cleared road by putting side of that big snow ball. It took more than a hour. We again had started journey and God had saved us from another land slide. We were informed that it was an area of Talibans and they could made us soft target if knew that we were media people from India.

Our bus was moving with slow speed. It was a hilly spiral roads and driver had to drive bus very cautiously. Slowly night was also passing. It was hard to sleep for all of us. Bus stopped at road side Dhaaba. We all took tea glasses in hands and started talking about the journey and this place. Dhaba (restaurant) owner called me and asked - Are you Indian ? I said - Yes, Then Dhaba owner advised me to leave this place immediately to remain safe from the danger of Talibans. Now we were thinking to cross that Talibanis area as early possible. Fear of Talibans had frozen our blood. We heard that Talibans don't fear even Pakistan Army. We had seen some of luxurious cars and vans loaded with arm and Talibans. We hardly breathe at that moment . We had heard about Talibani and this time were crossing from their region. Whenever we saw them, remembered our God to save us.

■■■

Chapter 42
Rawalpindi City

We had to reach Lahore via Rawalpindi while returning from Gilgit. And from Lahore we had to return our homeland. Our stunning and exciting journey from Gilgit to Rawalpindi via Karakoram was continued. Extreme of natural beauty took me into the stage of ecstasy. Nature had poured that much blessing on us but because of our greed we became enemy to one-another. Making of line of control, northern region, Pakistan occupied Kashmir or Azad Jammu and Kashmir, India's Kashmir, Land delivered to China all were making colas in the canvas of my memory. I was just thinking that India and Pakistan both the nations follow the tradition of Saints and Fakirs. Then why they allowed cropping up terrorist organizations like Taliban, Laskhar-e-taiba etc. These terrorist organizations have been working against humanity and can destroy its mentor nation Pakistan. History is witness of such examples where mentor of negative forces were destroyed by its products.

I found number of extremists in Pakistan were increasing every day, But why? Presence of extremists can make meaningless to all those liberal forces who are secular from mind and heart. I started humming lines of saint Bulle Shah

" Dhah De Mandir, Dhah De Masjid, Je Kuchh Dhenda Dhah De, Pyar Bhara Dil Kahin a Dhana, Jithe Rab Rehanda" (Distroy Temple, Mosque or whatever you want but never break a heart in love because God lives there.)

I came out from my thought when bus stopped at the portico of Hotel of Tourist Department at Rawalpindi. A long journey of approximate 900 kilometers had completed. I entered in my room in hotel, took a long bath to get fresh and

Army museum at Rawalpindi

came in hotel's lobby. It was the last destination of our visit and I wanted to use every second of it. Tomorrow we had to move towards our home land India. I had only few hours in hand. As I narrated in previous chapters that city Rawalpindi is a cantonment area. It is an army dominated city.

I wanted to see residence of General Parwej Musharraf. Though he was president of Pakistan yet favored to stay at his army quarter (Bunglow) at Rawalpindi. Residence of Parwej Musharraf was just like any other quarter of an army officer in an army cantonment. Yes I found additional security arrangement at the residence of General Parwej Musharraf. Whatever we met him, interacted with him and appreciated him. We all media person were influenced with his exterior attitude and personality.

As I told earlier that Rawalpindi and Islamabad are like twin city with opposite identity. Fast growing population will convert these two cities into one very soon.

History says that a city was developed in 19th century on the pass of world famous Grand Trunk Road (GT Road) and was named Rawalpindi. Islamabad is situated at the distance of 15 kilometers from Rawalpindi and this distance in being filled with growing population. Earlier Rawalpindi was under influence of Sikh Garrison and was an important business centre.

At present Rawalpindi is the head quarter of Army and known as a city of Army Cantonment.

Rawalpindi was also made a temporary capital city of newly born nation Pakistan. It served as a capital city of Pakistan till Islamabad got ready for this purpose.

You can see mini Pakistan in "Raja Bazar" (King Market) of Rawalpindi. An Army Museum situated in Raja Bazar will attract your attention. We could able to see spectacular Ayub National Park at Rawalpindi. This park was made in the memory of General Ayub Khan. It was spread in 900 hectares and decorated with gardens, spring falls etc. History says a lot of things about Rawalpindi.

It is also said that in 979-1030 AC, when Mohamood Gajnavi had attacked India repeatedly, this city was destroyed totally and Mahmood Gajnavi had awarded this city to one of his officer Gauhar.

Actually Rawalpindi was like a gate for attackers to enter into India and thus for many years this area remained without any population. Later in the year of 1493, Jhanda Khan captured this area and named one of village Rawal and in the course of times it became Rawalpindi. In 1765

Sikh captured this area. Whatever at present Rawalpindi carries a mix identity of both the ancient and modern face.

Now it was our last evening at Rawalpindi. I was seeing Residence of President General Parwej Mushrraf and felt an eye on me. I returned back to hotel. Though I knew about very famous Army museum at Rawalpindi but could not able to see it. Time has its wing and flies away

■■■

Chapter 43
Helpless Citizens of Pakistan

Next morning we had to return back. Fundamentalist and Separatist leaders started pouring into the hotel. It was almost a routine for them. They remained present on every possible place we visited. I clearly understood that Fundamentalists and separatist leaders had been informed about our every move by the ISI and they were supposed to deliver the bytes on the tune of the ISI. Though we all were tired but some of leaders wanted to talk with us. Just to maintain formality we talked to them. The outcome of their opinion had nothing different than discussed earlier. It all looked like sponsored program of the ISI. After dinner I shifted myself on bed. It was the last night. I went in thought process. A big nation was divided into parts and both the parts became enemy to each-other.

Even in Pakistan I experienced a huge difference between rich and poor. Common citizen of Pakistan are poor. Cities were full of beggars. They had migrated from remote and small villages in search of work and had started begging. Already I discussed briefly about beggars belonged to Muhajir families. In India also beggars are the common sight at red lights of various cities including capital city Delhi.

Corruption is the most discussed issue in India and also in Pakistan. According to Transparency International

Pakistani People after a horrible Incidence

corruption is at the top of Pakistan. People do mockery on corruption in Pakistan. They ask a question - "What is there on earth that never gets end apart from all the looting, exploiting, stealing. Answer comes as Pakistan.

Bribery, accepting gifts, taking commission in army contracts by army officers, scams by political leaders have become common phenomenon in Pakistan. Pakistan receives billions of Rupees as economic assistance by foreign countries specially from America and it is distributed to please all the powerful top people (leaders, army personnel, ISI....).

In 1999 General Parwej Musharraf toppled the democratic Government of Nawaj Sharif. To fight against corruption, first time in the history of Pakistan General Perwej Musharraf had formed National Accountability Bureau (NAB). This NAB had investigated almost about 1200 cases of corruption.

General Parwej Musharraf has written in his autobiography " Our economic system had collapsed and we were about to be bankrupt. Our leaders played great role in breaking institutional system and fearlessly remained in corruption, people at top Government posts were appointed by means corruption and it ruined the functioning of Government departments. Pakistan was engulfed from the top to bottom in corruption".

I knew with my experience that ten percent people of Pakistan were not corrupt and ten percent were habitually corrupt and rest of the eighty percent were acting according to prevailing situation. In all the public field 90 percent Government employee were engaged in corruption and were cheating nation at large.

President General Parwej Musharraf further writes in his autobiography that one could write an epic on the corruption in Pakistan. He gave an example. When he became President of Pakistan, attained a meeting in Sindh Governor's House. There he was discussing on budget of fixing a pipe line up to the sea for clearing sewage water and garbage. A presentation was demonstrated in front of him and other top officials. They gave a budget 116 billions rupees. Later they worked out again and put a budget of 75 billion rupees. General still considered this budget more than enough. He appointed a team of army engineers to calculate accurate budget to fixed proposed pipe line (Right bank out fall drain). Army engineers worked hard from March to August and reported General that it could be done in 16 billion rupees. They added some extra expenses and the final budget was drawn 18 billion rupees. Budget had come down from 116 billion rupees to just 18 billion rupees. General understood the reason behind making such budget. General Parwej Musharraf has mentioned many such incidence in his autobiography. We are also not less

An Encounter with Pakistan's Reality

than the Pakistan in corruption. During visit of Pakistan, few intellectuals told me that economy of Pakistan had remained in the hands of few people and this practice is continued since formation of Nation Pakistan. In 1959 only 222 people of Pakistan were doing business by taking huge loan from Banks.

In 1970, 66 percent of total industrial wealth were into the hands of only 22 families of Pakistan. These families had 70 percent share in insurance and 80 percent share in Banking. Top political parties like Pakistan people's party and Pakistan Muslim league had their top leaders and supporers from those families. These top families have been keeping their influence in Government, Army, the ISI, Police and all administrative works. They have their network everywhere. They are representatives of nation's wealth and it never matters for them that who runs the Government.

It always surprised me that why Pakistan could not able to adjust with its fundamentalist Muslims though it was born on the basis of religion. In 1971 one part of Pakistan became Bangladesh and rest of the Pakistan looked like divided in many segments. Why Pakistan don't look like a complete Nation ? General writes - " It is a matter of great sorrow that since 14 august 1947, Pakistan could not have an influential democracy. This is the basic reason of most of existing problems. The real meaning of democracy is a rule by the people and for the people. This has been forgotten. Intentionally Pakistan has been put under such administrative system that benefits only rich and corrupt people of the nation. They did not leave any scope for reforms. They have been producing tribal warriors, terrorists and fundamentalists. We Pakistani are divided into state, tribes. Caste, Sub-casts ,sects etc. We have got these things in inheritance. A good number of poor and backward population of Pakistan are also drug addicts. In Kabila's culture, drug is a common factor . From where they get Heroine, Ganja and Sulfa, no body wants to know.

Arms and ammunition are other common factor in most of the kabilie region. They carry AK-47 to all kinds of Pistol and Grenades. Government of Pakistan looks helpless to stop infiltration of arms to them. This is one of the bigger reason behind unstoppable terrorism in Pakistan. If you believe in data 2,50,000 arms were destroyed in April 2003 but why does Government of Pakistan not have any control on terrorists organization like Lashkar-e-Taiba, Jaish-e-Mohammed and its own ISI? They are directly responsible for supplying arms. This Pakistan visit had come with great experience. A journalist could not ask for more. Tomorrow we had to return India.

Thank you God, for creating such great Opportunity.

■■■

Chapter 44
Crossing Lahore Again

Here in India, we believe in Athithi Devo Bhava (Guest are like God) and Pakistan also follow the same culture. At least in caring and respecting guests both the nations have similar culture. We were returning back. Our bus were running on the motor way, one of finest road of Pakistan. This motor way connects Islamabad-Rawalpindi to Lahore. Both the sides of motor way were fenced with high iron net to stop animals from entering on the motor way. We saw vehicles of rangers doing patrolling on motor way for security reasons. Finest restaurants were opened to welcome guests, each after 40 to 50 kilometers. We have informed that this motor way had been constructed for taking off and landing of fighter planes during 1971 war. We were offered breakfast in a restaurant. We reached Lahore in the evening and were accommodated in a luxurious guest house Gulmohar. It was situated in a posh colony of Lahore.

I along with Nidhi, anchor of NDTV and cameraman Ajmat were making plan to buy some food items and were coming out from guest house. There we heard that some traditional singer (Mujrewali) were invited to entertain us. We ignored this information and went out. We reached in a big market, did shopping, ate some snacks in Mc-Donald and after two and half hour returned back in guest house.

Author along with a Pakistani Journalist at Lahore Rawalpindi Road

The moment we stepped inside hotel heard beautiful song with the sound of ghungroos. The programme of mujra (traditional dance) had already started. Here I must tell you that Lahore is the center of art and culture of Pakistan and culture of mujra (a traditional form of song & dance) is still alive there.

Actually one of our media friend unfolded his desire to see famous traditional dance (mujra) of Lahore that has been preserved here with great thirst.

I was surprised to see that in no time, they have arranged this programme. Lady dancer was combination of beauty, melodius voice and dance. Our some friends were loosing attire of life and discipline of the moment. Actually they were under influence of beauty and drink together. This program was arranged in hurry yet artist had given their best performance. It ended early than expected.

I was recalling a proverb "Jinna Lahore nahin Vekhya, O Janya hi hanin (You are not born if have not seen Lahore).

An Encounter with Pakistan's Reality

Motor Way connecting Lahore to Islamabad

Next day after a short good-bye meeting at press club Lahore, We had to return our nation. I was not getting sleep. Pictures of both of my Pakistan visit had come alive in my vision. With close eyes I was seeing a film on bigger canvas. It was a film of my memories. Sudden a scene came in my vision. The ISI people were trying to abduct me. I opened my eyes, took a glass of water and tried to get sleep.

With sound of Fazar (morning prayer at Mosque) I came out from bed, switched on TV, and got fresh. We took breakfast together and went to bow down our heads on the Shrine of Sufi Saint Data Sahib and on the Samadhi of Maharaja Ranjeet Singh. Now It was afternoon. We all with our luggage reached press club. It was the last moment of our visit. Press Club was full of journalists, officers and local leaders. Everybody had a hope for a better relationship between the two nations. President General Musharraf had send a note wishing all the best wishes to all of us. He also believed that Indo-Pakistani relationship will be better with the interactions at all level. We all took lunch at the Press club. Now it was the time when we said Good-bye to Pakistan. Our bus was moving to towards Bagha Border. We were returning back with great memories and hard facts. Some facts were unbelievable and some were inhuman and cruel.

Here again I quote Bulle Shah

"Apna Dass Tikana, Kidharo Aya Kidhar Jana.

Jis thane ka maan karen tun, ohnu naal na jana. Julm kare te lok satave, Kasab Fariyo lut khana,

Kar kai Chawar char Dihare Orak tun Uth jana,

Shahar Khamoshan de chal Basiya,

Dithe Mulak Samana.

(O' Creature, where you stay, from where you have come and where you have to go, your earned status, will not go with you in heaven. You do crime and torture people. O' dear, don't have ego, one day you have to go from this earth.)

■ ■ ■